Reflections

Reflections

My Life in the Deaf and Hearing Worlds

John B. Christiansen

Gallaudet University Press
Washington, D.C.

Gallaudet University Press
Washington, D.C. 20002
http://gupress.gallaudet.edu

Library of Congress Cataloging-in-Publication Data

Christiansen, John B.
   Reflections : my life in the deaf and hearing worlds / John B. Christiansen.
      p. cm.
   Includes bibliographical references.
   ISBN-13: 978-1-56368-477-7
   ISBN-10: 1-56368-477-2
   1. Christiansen, John B.   2. Deaf—United States—Biography.
   3. College teachers—United States—Biography.   4. Cochlear implants—
   United States.   I. Title.
   HV2534.C47A3 2010
   362.4'2092—dc22
   [B]
                                                        2010038056

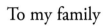
To my family

Contents

Preface

THIS BOOK GREW OUT of my personal experiences as an academic sociologist and as a lifelong hard of hearing and deaf person. I have spent more than thirty years as a card-carrying member of the former and more than sixty years as part of the latter (sans membership card but, I assume, in good standing in the eyes of whoever is keeping track).

I make no claim to speak for any of the other 30 million or so people in the United States with some degree of hearing loss, nor am I presumptuous enough to think that my experiences are special or that I have unique insights into problems faced by deaf and hard of hearing people. So, one might reasonably ask, why write a book about the subject?

For one thing, I have time and I like to write. I spent thirty-two years teaching deaf and hard of hearing students (and a few hearing ones as well) at Gallaudet University in Washington, D.C., before retiring in August 2009. During that span, I wrote the articles, chapters, books, book reviews, and other publications that are traditionally expected of college professors. Some of them actually may have been read, although I definitely have not become rich on the royalties. Since I'm in good health and see few more attractive alternatives on the immediate retirement horizon, writing another book seemed like a promising proposition.

Of course, a writer must also have something worthwhile to write about. Over the years, I've read quite a few memoirs written by deaf and hard of hearing people, and I will refer to many of these books in the pages that follow. However, as far as I can tell, none of these books have been written by a sociologist (certainly not by a sociologist with a cochlear implant), and I thought I could add a perspective that is largely absent in the literature. In addition, I'm a "both/and" person when it comes to being deaf and hard of hearing, not an "either/or" person. That is, I've had experiences with a relatively mild to moderate, high-frequency hearing loss, experiences with more severe hearing loss, and experiences with profound deafness. Over the years, I've used no hearing aids, one hearing aid, two hearing aids, and, at present, a cochlear implant. Because of the nature of cochlear implant surgery and because of a progressive hearing loss in my nonimplanted ear, I am a deaf person when not using my implant. When I am using the device, I'm a hard of hearing person. As one might surmise, this can be a bit confusing at times, both for me and for others (just ask my wife, Arlene, or my children and friends). Some of my experiences growing up as a deaf person, a hard of hearing person, and a person with a cochlear implant are discussed in the first two chapters of this book. There is some overlap, but I have tried to keep most of the implant material in the second chapter.

During the last decade of my career at Gallaudet, I did a fair amount of research (often with colleagues) related to cochlear implants, especially pediatric implants, and I will offer some thoughts on that topic at the end of the second chapter. Although these observations are my own, they are based primarily on academic research and scholarship, not on my own experiences as a cochlear implant user.

At Gallaudet, I participated in several search committees, the most recent of which was the search for the ninth president of the university in 2006. As many readers may know, this was a very traumatic time for the university; in fact, Gallaudet experienced the second major protest in less than twenty years over the selection of a new president. In some respects, the protest of 2006 was more emotional, and certainly more divisive on campus, than the Deaf President Now (DPN) revolution in 1988. My reflections on the 2006 protest are discussed in the third chapter. This chapter focuses primarily on one event rather than on a series of personal experiences that occurred over an extended period of time. It is included in this volume for two reasons. First, it is an interesting and fascinating event that warrants description and explanation. Although the conflict occurred at Gallaudet University, many of the issues raised during the protest resonate far beyond the gates of the campus. In addition, the 2006 protest in some ways represents a continuation of the story of one person's never-ending navigation among many of the conflicts and challenges discussed or alluded to in the first two chapters: deaf versus hard of hearing versus hearing, American Sign Language (ASL) versus English versus bilingualism, and "deaf enough" versus "not deaf enough." As such, the final chapter brings many of the themes and issues mentioned in the first two chapters to a denouement.

Who might find this book helpful or worth reading? First, I hope that many of my deaf and hard of hearing friends and colleagues, as well as other deaf and hard of hearing people, might find something useful or interesting in my comments and observations. In addition, and equally important, I hope that many friends, family members, and acquaintances of those who have some degree of hearing loss might develop a greater appreciation of some of the problems and issues that we grapple with on a daily basis.

Part I.

Baseball, Toothbrush, Hot Dog, Airplane: Life as a Deaf and Hard of Hearing Person

The Angel Chime

MANY READERS WILL RECOGNIZE the words *baseball, toothbrush, hot dog,* and *airplane.* Audiologists, listening therapists, and others typically use these and other two-syllable words to determine speech reception threshold, which is the softest or faintest level of speech that someone can hear and consistently understand. Because I have undergone countless hearing tests and have heard these words repeated dozens of times in a variety of settings, they have become my metaphor for the challenges, as well as the opportunities, of having a hearing loss.

Many people with some degree of hearing loss in their life have written books about their experiences. These include David Wright, whose book *Deafness* is widely seen as a classic in the field, and Henry Kisor, the author of *What's That Pig Outdoors?*[1] Wright and Kisor are both part of the "oral tradition" among deaf people; neither learned to sign and both lived in the hearing world. Neither would be considered part of the Deaf community, either in England, where Wright, a South African poet, spent most of his life, or in Illinois and Michigan, where Kisor, the retired book editor for the *Chicago Sun-Times*, resides. Another account, written as diary entries that span the 1990s, is *A Quiet World*. In this book, hard of hearing psychologist David Myers describes how he adjusted to using a hearing aid and to his progressive hearing loss.[2]

Other autobiographical accounts reflect the tradition of culturally deaf (Deaf) people who use sign communication, usually American Sign Language (ASL).* Among the noteworthy contributions here are Gina Oliva's story, *Alone in the Mainstream*, and some of the other books in Gallaudet University Press's Deaf Lives series. Also included in this tradition are books written by children of Deaf adults (Codas), who, although hearing, grew up with parents in the Deaf community. Important contributions are Lou Ann Walker's *A Loss for Words*, R. H. Miller's *Deaf Hearing Boy*, and Paul Preston's *Mother Father Deaf*.[3]

In addition to these accounts, several people who have received a cochlear implant have discussed how they have adjusted to life as a user and the difference this has made in their everyday activities. One interesting and informative book is *Rebuilt* by Michael Chorost. Others include Arlene Romoff's *Hear Again*, which is also in the form of a diary, and Beverly Biderman's *Wired for Sound*.[4]

Josh Swiller's *The Unheard* is a fascinating account of his life as a deaf person, especially his experiences as a Peace Corps volunteer in Zambia. Although Swiller received a cochlear implant, he does not discuss that experience in his memoir.[5]

Which of these traditions do I identify with? Am I part of the oral tradition, where lipreading and listening skills are emphasized? Or do I identify more closely with those who are part of the Deaf community and use ASL? What about the loosely defined but growing cochlear

---

*Following convention, uppercase Deaf refers to people who identify with the Deaf community, frequently associate with other Deaf people, and are reasonably fluent in ASL. Lowercase deaf refers to people with an audiological condition usually characterized by a severe to profound hearing loss.

implant community? The best answer is "all of the above." I grew up as a hard of hearing person who had almost no contact with deaf or Deaf people until I was thirty. In fact, I had not even heard of Gallaudet College (now University) until I was looking for a job during my last year of graduate school, and I had never seen a sign language interpreter. Now, more than thirty years later, I am reasonably fluent in ASL. Whatever else I've done in my life, I certainly have experienced many different ways of being deaf and hard of hearing.

—*m*—

As far as anyone knows, I was not hard of hearing as an infant. In fact, according to family lore, the first time anyone noticed my hearing loss was when I was about five or six years old. This event took place around Christmas when my family, including relatives, was sitting around a table listening to the sounds made by a Christmas angel centerpiece. This gold-colored tin angel chime is still available today, and we have one at home that we occasionally dust off in December. There are four three-inch-long candles on a small circular base. When these candles are lit, an angel, catching the updraft, begins to spin, and small hard wires attached to the angel repeatedly strike the two bells that are part of the centerpiece. The high-frequency sound is quite soft. Everyone around the table that Christmas was saying how beautiful it was, except for me, because I was not able to hear the sounds.

One question people ask frequently when a physical condition not considered "normal" occurs is "why?": Why is my child deaf or hard of hearing? What could I, as a parent, have done to cause this to happen? What did the doctors do wrong? Explanations include spinal meningitis, another childhood illness accompanied by a high fever, accidents, maternal rubella, and various genetic etiologies.[6] Perhaps surprisingly in this day and age, a common answer is still "we don't know." So it was for me. I did have the usual litany of mid-twentieth-century childhood diseases, including the mumps and chicken pox. It is possible that my hearing loss is a result of one of these illnesses. I also had my tonsils and adenoids removed as a child, another common medical rite of passage for many people in my generation. Perhaps some undetected complication from that surgery, an infection perhaps, led to the progressive loss that I've experienced. Perhaps there is another reason. At this stage of my life, I suspect that I'll never know. Like many deaf and hard of hearing people, as well as many parents of deaf children, I don't spend a lot of time thinking about this since it makes little practical difference in terms of choosing among the variety of educational and communication strategies, as well as among the various technologies, that are available.

I don't recall much of what happened in the years immediately after the revealing moment with the angel chime, except for the fact that one of my aunts, Grace Christiansen, happened to be a teacher of deaf children in Stevens Point, Wisconsin. Like many schools for deaf kids in the mid-twentieth century, this school practiced an oral method of instruction. Aunt Grace did not use any form of sign communication; lipreading and using residual hearing were emphasized. Because I was hard of hearing and could hear most voices reasonably well, I tried some lipreading training and speech practice with her during the summer. No one suggested that I learn how to sign; no one considered it necessary, and in fact, it was not something I even knew about.

For most of the year, my parents and my younger brother David and I lived in Salt Lake City, Utah, but almost every summer we drove fifteen hundred miles on pre-interstate highways to my paternal grandparents' home about forty miles north of Milwaukee, Wisconsin. The house, which everyone called the "ramshack," sat on the shore of Lake Michigan near the small town of Cedar Grove. Cousins came to visit, other friends and relatives were always around, and water sports and swimming took up much of our time. Consequently, my lipreading training with Aunt Grace often was relegated to the proverbial back burner. One positive result of this training involved my own speech. I had a noticeable lisp as a youngster, and because I've long since learned how to say my *s* sounds and other difficult-to-hear consonants correctly,

With my younger brother Dave, December 1952.

I'm sure my limited work with Aunt Grace was both productive and worthwhile. I'm also a reasonably good lipreader, and I have my aunt to thank for much of this ability as well.

Salt Lake City

My early childhood experiences in Salt Lake City were not exceptional, although some were no doubt unique to a hard of hearing son of a Presbyterian minister and his wife. My parents, Don and Betty Christiansen, had moved to Salt Lake from Milwaukee in 1946, a few months after I was born. My parents had served as missionaries in Ketchikan, Alaska, for five years before World War II. Soon after the war started, my father enlisted in the Army Air Corps as a chaplain, and my parents lived at air force bases near Dayton, Ohio, and Macon, Georgia, before finding their way to the Salt Lake Valley. Protestants were scarce in Utah in the 1940s, even more so than they are today, and my parents were deeply involved in helping the newly formed Wasatch Presbyterian Church develop into one of the largest Protestant congregations in the state.

Neither of my parents had much experience with deaf or hard of hearing people, and I recall only fleeting contact with any deaf people as I was growing up. Two Deaf people I do recall meeting were old acquaintances of my parents from Iowa. I'm not sure how my parents came to know them or how they communicated with them, but they stayed with us for a few days while they were visiting Salt Lake. I must have been about ten years old when this couple visited us, and I had little interaction with them. In fact, I had no clue how to communicate with them.

Some fifty years later, the fact that their names came up in an un-related situation says a great deal about the remarkable cohesiveness of the Deaf community in America. I was having lunch in the snack bar at Gallaudet University one day when Ron Sutcliffe, a retired faculty member, approached me and said that he had gone to school in Iowa with two friends, had heard from them recently, and said they wanted him to say hello to me. I didn't remember their names but did remember the couple who had visited with us. How they remembered me from their visit to Salt Lake, or how they even knew I was at Gallaudet, I have no idea. Perhaps my parents had told them I was hard of hearing when they visited us and they remembered this, or perhaps they simply recognized my name in a Gallaudet publication.

—*rrm*—

I attended three different elementary schools in Salt Lake, including one that started about seven o'clock in the morning. Such an early start was not something that my friends and I looked forward to, but in the days when baby boom children in a state with a very high birthrate were flooding the school system, at least some of the public schools in Salt Lake had to operate two shifts. I don't recall being asked which shift I preferred, but it was nice to have my weekday afternoons free, particularly when the weather was warm.

My public school experiences long predated Public Law 94-142, the Education for All Handicapped Children Act, which was enacted in the mid-1970s (and renamed the Individuals with Disabilities Education Act—IDEA—about fifteen years later). Among other things, this legislation requires "free and appropriate public educational services" for children with disabilities. Even though this was not the law when I attended school, I did receive a small number of school-based services. The most obvious one at my repeated request and sometimes the more vocal request of my parents was to be seated at the front of the room and to be in a class where the teacher spoke clearly. I also was seen periodically by a speech therapist in lieu of attending music classes while I was in elementary school. Music classes were difficult for me in the days before assistive listening devices or other forms of classroom amplification were used and before creative music teachers emphasized movement and playing instruments, not just sitting around singing songs. Most of the therapy consisted of listening to various war stories the therapist, a World War II veteran, told during these sessions. I don't think this speech therapy lasted for more than a year, but the experience is somewhat ironic because my wife Arlene was a dynamic and creative elementary school music teacher who focused on movement and having the children play sophisticated musical instruments such as recorders, glockenspiels, and xylophones. Moreover, with my cochlear implant, I now enjoy listening to many types of music, especially modern and classical jazz, Japanese taiko drums, and Spanish flamenco.

Baseball

As a youngster, I was especially into baseball and, in my wholly objective assessment, was quite good at it, at least during the little league years when I was between nine and twelve. (In Salt Lake City, this was not the formal Little League but something called the Western Boys Baseball Association.) I was a bit chubby and tall, played first base, hit a lot of home runs, and made the all-star team. This brought a certain amount of status, which I enjoyed. We also played pickup baseball games in our neighborhood and frequently played late into the summer nights.

At that age, baseball skills (and athletic ability in general) counted for quite a lot in the adolescent pecking order, and whatever communication difficulties I faced as a hard of hearing youngster were typically ignored or quickly forgotten, especially after I hit a few home runs. Although not of major importance, communication issues were not completely absent on the ball field. The first time my hearing loss became an issue while playing organized baseball was when, as a nascent nine-year-old, I was in right field (the usual position for first-year players) and collided with the center fielder as we were both running to catch a fly ball. I had not heard my teammate yell, "I got it," and we all became conscious of the need to communicate more clearly on the field. This incident had little lasting significance beyond that, however, since my hearing was still good enough for me to communicate in most situations with my friends, teammates, and coaches. Even though I was hard of hearing, that aspect of my identity did not become a major issue when I was a young adolescent, especially when I was involved in sports.

One of the highlights of my little league years came early one spring morning when a friend and I, fully decked out in our baseball uniforms, strolled around the restaurant of a fancy local hotel and asked the major league players who were having breakfast there for their autographs. The players were in Salt Lake to participate in one of the last games of spring training before the major league season began a few days later. The team was the 1956 (or perhaps 1957) New York Giants, a team that had won the World Series in 1954. As every older baseball fan knows, the star of that team was the incomparable Willie Mays. My friend's mother, who worked at the hotel, arranged for this experience. My friend and I each had a new baseball for the players to autograph as we circled around the room, interrupting them while they were eating. I even had the chutzpah to ask one of the players—Wes Westrum, the catcher—what his name was because I couldn't read his handwriting. Fortunately for me, I heard him mumble "Westrum" the first time and didn't have to ask him to repeat it. The highlight of the morning came when we were ready to leave: Mays, the "Say Hey Kid" himself, emerged from the elevator in his slippers and signed the balls for us. Unfortunately, I have no idea where the autographed baseball is now—its value would probably support me in grand style in my retirement.

—*mm*—

Following little league, there were basically two baseball options in Salt Lake. One was the so-called Cops League and the other was the Babe Ruth League. I don't recall why one of the leagues was called Cops, but presumably the police department sponsored the program. Like many of my friends, I tried out for both leagues, fully expecting to be selected by a team in each league.

The tryouts for the Cops League occurred first. After they were over, there was a general meeting on the baseball field, and each team's manager read the names of the boys who had been selected for their team. There were at least five or six teams. I was not selected on the first team, or the second, or the third . . . and I became puzzled. I found it hard to believe that they wouldn't pick me; after all, I had led my little league in home runs the year before. Surely someone knew that! But after all the teams had been announced, there I was sitting on the bench, almost by myself. I couldn't believe it. That was more than fifty years ago, and I still remember crying my eyes out as I slowly walked home (it was a long walk) and wondering what I was going to do next. In fact, I walked and stumbled right into my father's office at our church, perhaps seeking some type of divine, or at least paternal, intervention.

So much for the Cops League; at least the Babe Ruth League was left. Lucky for me, I was selected for a team in the Babe Ruth League, a league that was obviously much better than the Cops. In fact, one of my friends who had been selected for teams in both leagues decided to join the team playing on a real baseball diamond. (The Cops League didn't play on a full-size field.) I was not a star on my team as a thirteen-year-old, but I got some hits and some playing time in the outfield and at first base. I also lost some weight, something that the manager of the team strongly suggested I do.

My major league prospects took a turn for the worse the next year when I decided to spend the summer in Wisconsin, at the ramshack, playing golf and working around the huge yard (where I designed my own miniature golf course). I also had time to get some speech and lipreading therapy from Aunt Grace. I still thought I was a pretty good baseball player, however, and tried out for my high school team a year or so later, which proved to be Cops League déjà vu all over again (although I didn't cry, at least not all the way home, this time).

I was surprised that I wasn't chosen for the baseball team in high school. It is certainly possible that I was not as good as I thought I was and that the other guys were better. However, I think it is entirely possible that my hearing loss had something to do with it. Baseball is played on a big field, and with managers and coaches yelling instructions from one end to the other, it is certainly possible that I missed hearing their instructions. Moreover, there was no way I would have known that I had missed something. If, for example, they yelled at me to "hit the cut-off man" while I was in center field 250 feet away, and I threw it to the wrong base or over the guy's head, the obvious conclusion was that I wasn't paying attention or didn't even know what a cut-off man was.

I must admit that I didn't come up with this air-tight explanation until recently. At the time, in high school, it wasn't cool to tell everyone that I was hard of hearing (not that it was particularly cool to make this an issue in elementary or junior high school, either). I had to tell the teachers, or at least give them a note from my parents, because I wanted to sit in the front, but otherwise I wasn't eager to spread the word. I had been told by the ear, nose, and throat specialist that I had been seeing off and on since the encounter with the Christmas angel chime that a hearing aid would not be useful for me. I don't know if that assessment was accurate for the type of hearing loss I had—I could hear lower frequencies fairly well but not the higher ones. However, because I wasn't anxious to have an aid, I wasn't about to argue with him. (I have what is called a *sensorineural hearing loss*, a term I didn't know existed until much later; at the time, I was simply told I had "nerve deafness.")

A few years ago I was reading Gina Oliva's book, *Alone in the Mainstream*. Part of the book includes her account of her formative years as a deaf girl growing up in Connecticut. One thing Gina and I have in common is that we are both still quite active. (Gina was a physical education professor at Gallaudet until her retirement in 2009, and although my baseball-playing days are long gone, I'm always on the lookout for opportunities to ride my bicycle—more on that later.) In her book, Gina describes the same kind of thing I recall experiencing as a frustrated adolescent baseball player: not getting chosen for a school team and wondering why, especially since she, like me, had usually been selected first for sports teams when she was younger. Gina attributed her exclusion, at least in part, to communication difficulties and perhaps missing something important along the way. Talk about the proverbial light bulb going on in my head! This must be at least part of the explanation for my truncated high school athletic career. What could I have done differently? Why didn't I think of that explanation in high school and do something about it?

—*mm*—

Questions like this have come up consistently throughout my life. Judging from the conversations I've had with other deaf and hard of hearing people as well as some of the memoirs they have written, these kinds of questions are fairly typical for those of us with a hearing loss. After mentioning a few more of my experiences, I will discuss some sociological concepts and insights that might help explain the reluctance to "do something" that many people experience when faced with ambiguous and frustrating communication situations. Although this reluctance is sometimes difficult to deal with, there are nevertheless some situations that can be structured or changed in ways to make communication easier and more rewarding.

~~~~

While this is getting a bit ahead of the story, my baseball career did end on a happy note, but not until my junior year of college, when I took advantage of a junior year abroad program and attended Silliman University in the Philippines. I played on the varsity baseball team and, with all due modesty, helped lead our team to a very successful season. It was also a wonderful opportunity to travel to different cities in the Philippines. Was communication a problem there? No doubt, but communication was a bit of a problem for all of us from outside the Philippines, and people didn't take trouble-free interaction and communication for granted.* By then I was wearing a hearing aid, and most of my friends and acquaintances knew I was hard of hearing.

Perhaps one thing I might have done differently to satisfy my high school athletic aspirations would have been to focus on individual rather than team sports. Certainly, sports such as golf, tennis, and track didn't have the status that team sports such as football and basketball had, but communication difficulties might not have been such an issue in these sports. In addition, there is less subjectivity involved in deciding who makes the team: the lowest scores in golf, the best times or the longest distances in track and field, and the most victories in tennis. Given my

---

*In this sense, my experiences in the Philippines were similar to Josh Swiller's experiences in Zambia, which he recounts in *The Unheard*. Although Swiller was in the Peace Corps and I was a college student, we both discovered that being deaf or hard of hearing was not a big deal when everyone was by necessity more conscious of communication issues and when people were obliged to take more time to make sure they understood each other.

quarter-century obsession with cycling, maybe that would have been a good choice, except for the unfortunate fact that we didn't live in France (where the Tour de France takes place) and few people in America knew much about bicycle racing before Lance Armstrong and Greg LeMond won the Tour. Another drawback for many individual sports, especially golf and tennis, is that they require a lot of practice and instruction. When I was in high school, this was typically available at country clubs, which we were in no position to afford.

An "Awful Incertitude"

If my adolescent, post–little league athletic career was largely characterized by unfulfilled ambition, what about the rest of my life during these formative years? At the very least, my status as a hard of hearing kid made life more difficult than if I had been either deaf or hearing. Moreover, the phrase *hard of hearing* itself is very ambiguous. One can have a mild or moderate hearing loss or a hearing loss that is quite pronounced. In both cases, the label *hard of hearing* is generally used to describe the conditions. In actuality, life for someone who can readily communicate on the phone, for example, which someone who is mildly hard of hearing can do, is quite different from life for one who can't.

When I was a teenager, I had enough residual hearing to hear well enough on the phone to call friends, including girlfriends (potential or actual), to talk or ask them out on a date. For me, it was much easier to hear on the phone, where only two people were trying to understand each other, than at a noisy party. My experience in this regard is quite different from that of Henry Kisor, who recounts in his book *What's That Pig Outdoors?* that because he couldn't hear on the phone he had to ask his mother or father, and later his sister, to call and try to arrange dates for him. Needless to say, he wasn't too thrilled with this arrangement. I didn't have a sister, so I couldn't have used his approach in any case (my brother, who is three years younger than I am, would not have been a good option), and I can't imagine having to ask one of my parents to do the job for me. As a hard of hearing kid, at least I

Degrees and Types of Hearing Loss

The terms *mild, moderate, severe,* and *profound* are frequently used to roughly delineate different degrees of hearing loss. A mild hearing loss means that a person might have difficulty following conversations, particularly in a relatively noisy setting, often without using a hearing aid. A person with a moderate hearing loss probably would need to turn up the volume on a television or a telephone and would almost certainly benefit from using a hearing aid. A person with a moderate hearing loss might also benefit from closed captions on television programs. A severe hearing loss means that the person needs a powerful hearing aid and will likely have considerable difficulty understanding conversations without lipreading, especially in noisy situations. Many people with a moderate to severe hearing loss are candidates for cochlear implants, especially if they do not derive much benefit from using a hearing aid. People with a profound hearing loss can hear only extremely loud sounds, such as a lawnmower or fire truck, without amplification. Given the likelihood of poor discrimination ability even with an aid, most individuals in this category would be candidates for implants.

More technically, a person who is moderately hard of hearing might be described as having a 50-dB (decibel) average hearing loss, whereas a person who is severely hard of hearing might have a 90-dB loss. This means that if a person with "normal" hearing can hear a sound (a dripping faucet, for example) at 20 dB (very soft), it would require amplification to 50 dB for a person who is moderately hard of hearing to hear the same sound and amplification to 90 dB for a person with a severe hearing loss to hear the sound. It is important to keep in mind that because the decibel scale is logarithmic, rather than linear, each 10-dB increase corresponds to a *tenfold* increase in sound pressure level. That is, a sound at 50 dB is 1,000 times greater than a sound at 20 dB ($10 \times 10 \times 10$). In this example, for a person with a moderate hearing loss to hear the dripping faucet, the sound would have to be 1,000 times greater than it needs to be for a person without a hearing loss. And for a person with a 90-dB hearing loss? The sound of the dripping faucet would have to be 10 million times greater—that is, more intense—for the person to be able to hear it ($10 \times 10 \times 10 \times 10 \times 10 \times 10 \times 10$).

In addition to these different degrees of hearing loss, there are also several different types of hearing loss, including *conductive, sensorineural,* and *mixed.* A conductive hearing loss occurs because of a problem in the outer or middle ear that interferes with the transmission or conduction of sound waves to the inner ear. This type of hearing loss is frequently mild or moderate and often can be corrected by surgery or by draining fluid from the ear. A sensorineural hearing loss, which is caused by damage within the cochlea—especially damage to the thousands of microscopic hair cells in the cochlea or to the acoustic nerve linking the cochlea to the brain—is permanent and usually cannot be corrected by surgery. A sensorineural loss can range from mild to profound. A mixed hearing loss would be a combination of both conductive and sensorineural types of hearing loss.

had more flexibility and freedom in this regard than Kisor, a nonsigning deaf person, did.

If I had been either deaf or hearing, my status would not have been in doubt. Of course, if I had been severely hard of hearing or profoundly deaf as a youngster, there still would have been the question of what type of educational and communication strategies to use, where to attend school, and so on. But at least it would have been clear that I was not "hearing only what I wanted to hear," as some people accused me of doing. As David Wright writes in his memoir, *Deafness,* in some ways, "the partially deaf . . . have the worst of both worlds."

I think, too, that embarrassing social situations, missed conversations, awkward silences at parties and other occasions inevitably had a dampening effect on my self-confidence. I still recall a time in junior high school when I was walking in the hall and one of the prettiest girls in the school said, "Hi, John," to me. Not quite sure I really heard what I thought I heard, I momentarily didn't say anything in return. Alas, by the time I figured out what I thought she had said, it was too late for me to say anything. The next thing I thought I heard was "stuck up," presumably what she said after getting no response from me. And then there were the parties and dances in high school, which usually took place under less than ideal lighting and acoustical conditions. For example, once I was with a small group of friends at a dance and I managed to figure out that they were talking about the "Y." I innocently asked which YMCA they were talking about. This happened to be the wrong Y, an error that should have been obvious to me even before I got the usual assortment of puzzled looks from my friends. This being Utah, they were talking about BYU (Brigham Young University).

Issues and situations like these are recurrent themes in many of the memoirs written by deaf and hard of hearing people. Making inappropriate comments as a consequence of not being able to clearly follow the conversation, social isolation, and the "awful incertitude" (to use David Wright's poignant phrase) of not knowing what is going on are problems that many deaf or hard of hearing people have to deal with on a regular basis. Many of those who have written about these matters tend to put the blame for instances of failed communication squarely on their own shoulders. Although I agree that much of the responsibility does, in fact, lie with the deaf or hard of hearing person in this regard, it is equally important to focus on social and cultural factors in an attempt to explain why problems such as these continue to occur.

In any case, split-second conversational decisions that people are faced with on a daily basis are frequently difficult for deaf and hard of hearing people to make. This is because we may not be sure what we thought we heard is what the speaker actually said, and we have to momentarily weigh a number of alternative scenarios before deciding how to respond. This takes a little time, and, by the time we have sorted through the various alternatives, the conversation has often moved on to another topic.

The Looking-Glass Self

As I grew older, it became increasingly apparent to me that there was often a poor fit between what I thought about myself and what others thought about me. I continue to have an image of myself as a reasonably friendly and outgoing person (as my daughter Amanda, who is no doubt totally objective in these matters, reminds me). However, many of my former high school friends and classmates, in the unlikely event they remember me at all, might not see me that way. This would be perfectly understandable. The guy sitting quietly on the sofa, or off in the corner during a party and not contributing much besides some embarrassed head nodding and an occasional and often irrelevant comment is not likely to be invited back to many parties. In such situations, good friends in elementary school or junior high (middle) school have a way of becoming more difficult to stay in contact with by the time high school rolls around.

Sociologists often talk and write about something called the *looking-glass self*, a concept associated with the late Charles Cooley, who taught for many years at the University of Michigan. *Looking-glass* is another term for a mirror, but in a sociologist's conceptualization, a looking-glass is one's audience, typically friends, classmates, family, and coworkers, not an actual mirror. In this perspective, our feelings about ourselves, our self-image as it were, are based to a great extent on what we think others think about us, how we perceive ourselves as reflected in the reactions of others. If we believe others think well of us, this naturally makes us feel pretty good about ourselves. If we think they don't, the opposite is likely to occur. What's important here is our perception of what others think about us, not how they might really feel.

For many deaf and hard of hearing people, there is often a bad fit between the image we have of ourselves and the image other people may have about us (or, more precisely, the image we think other people have about us). I'm sure this observation is true for many other people as well. For example, a well-educated, well-dressed, professional African American man who can't get a taxi may experience a dissonance between his image of himself and the cab driver's perception. No doubt many people with disabilities that are more visible than being deaf or hard of hearing have similar experiences.[7]

What, if anything, can be done about this? What could I have done differently, growing up as a hard of hearing child? What can any "non-standard" person do to make everyday situations more positive and less frustrating? What can parents do to make life a little easier for their deaf or hard of hearing child? Here, again, sociology has something useful to say.

The Power of Positive Situations

Rev. Norman Vincent Peale was not a sociologist, but he did write an influential book many years ago entitled *The Power of Positive Thinking*. Although positive thinking is certainly better than negative thinking, or not thinking at all, one thing that sociology has emphasized over the years is what might be called "the power of positive situations." That is to say, it is important not only for people to change their thoughts but also for situations to be structured, and changed if necessary, to promote actions that can lead to more positive and productive attitudes. A classic example is the civil rights movement and legislation that accompanied that effort. For instance, in the 1950s and early 1960s, before the Civil Rights Act of 1964 and the Voting Rights Act of 1965 and other civil rights legislation became law, there was very little support for marriage between white and black people in the United States. (In some states, antimiscegenation laws made such marriages illegal until the Supreme Court declared otherwise in 1967.) Today, there is much less opposition. According to the Gallup poll, which has been tracking this issue since the 1950s, in 1958 only 4 percent of whites approved of such interracial marriages; by 2007, this had increased to 77 percent. This change wasn't simply the result of people having more positive thoughts or pleas from religious and moral leaders encouraging people to love or at least get along with one another. Rather, this transformation was to a great extent the result of modifications in laws and practices that eventually led to changes in attitudes. Legislating morality, or changing the culture, is a slow process, perhaps, but a powerful one.*

How might this apply to a deaf or hard of hearing child? Or to another kid with a physical impairment that leads to a disabling situation? It is not only the physical condition itself that is the problem, but also the nature of the situation in which those with the condition typically find themselves. Changing the situation or the environment, especially for children and adolescents, is easier said than done, but considerable progress has been made in this regard during the past quarter-century. For example, Public Law 94-142, mentioned earlier, has led to a massive mainstreaming movement resulting in the inclusion of thousands of children with disabilities into regular classrooms in our public schools. Although certainly not without problems or controversies (many Deaf people prefer educational programs in traditional residential schools because of the special visual needs of deaf and hard of hearing children, and sometimes the integration of children with disabilities into mainstreamed classrooms is far less than ideal), the very fact that kids without special needs are interacting with children with such needs on a regular, day-to-day basis can't help but lead to more positive attitudes. My wife Arlene taught for many years in a public elementary school that had dozens of children with disabilities integrated into regular classrooms. These kids often need special accommodations, but that is what the law requires, and for the other children who grow up in this setting this integration is a natural part of the social and cultural landscape in their elementary school.

---

*Daniel Patrick Moynihan, who is perhaps better known as a former U.S. senator from New York than as a former sociologist, had this to say about legislating morality in a frequently quoted aphorism: "The central conservative truth is that it is culture, not politics, that determines the success of a society. The central liberal truth is that politics can change a culture and save it from itself." Legislating morality—or trying to change behavior and attitudes by changing laws—is not invariably successful, as the failed effort to ban alcohol sales and consumption in the U.S. during the Prohibition era (1919–33) reminds us.

In and Out of the Classroom

Although situations can be changed to promote more positive outcomes, there is still a wide gap between what happens in the classroom and what happens in other environments, where friendships are formed and more intimate relationships develop. It is one thing to require that classrooms have amplification systems, that sign language interpreters be available when requested, that hard of hearing students be given preference for seats in the front of the room, that kids raise their hands and take turns while talking, and so on. It is a very different thing to require any of this at recess, in the lunchroom, or at parties or dances. The most frustrating times for me during my formative years were not in the classroom. If I missed something there, as I often did, I usually knew enough to look it up myself or ask the teacher for help after class. Although teachers varied tremendously in their willingness to take time to answer my questions, I was at least able to keep up with my peers in the classroom without too much trouble. Nevertheless, while my grades were reasonably good, I've often wondered if they could have been even better if I had had the type of services in school that many deaf and hard of hearing students, as well as other students with disabilities, have today.

One of the themes in David Wright's book *Deafness* is his observation that it is often difficult for deaf people to fill in the gaps in common knowledge and experience ("the fund of miscellaneous and temporary useless information") that others may pick up unconsciously, simply by overhearing what people say. Although it was indeed difficult for me to pick up information, useless or not, by overhearing—or sometimes just hearing—what others were saying, I was able to partially compensate for this by developing an early love of reading for pleasure. For this, I thank my parents who, over the years, had accumulated hundreds of issues of old *Reader's Digest* magazines. As a young child, I spent countless hours reading the condensed articles from these magazines as well as increasing my vocabulary by diligently going through the quizzes designed to increase one's "word power." Over the years, the habit of reading something before I believed it has been quite useful. Whatever academic success I've enjoyed over the years, including the need to look up things that I missed in the classroom, can be attributed, in no small part, to my early reading experiences and my voracious reading habit.

———

Classroom situations were often frustrating, and I frequently found myself in predicaments I didn't know how to handle. For example, in one class when I was a senior in high school, the class was listening to a recording of a comedy monologue by Jonathan Winters. I'm not sure what this monologue had to do with the class, but everyone around me was laughing hysterically at his jokes, and I couldn't make out a thing he was saying. What was I supposed to do? Maybe I should have complained to the teacher or to the principal that this was a pretty poor use of class time, but for some reason I didn't think of that at the time (and I'm sure I wouldn't have had the guts to do it even if I had). Perhaps I could have asked someone to repeat the jokes to me, but that didn't seem like a promising approach either. Maybe I could have asked the teacher to turn the sound up, but I doubt if that would have done much good. In short, I didn't see any good options here, except to feign interest in the recording and pretend to laugh when I saw others laughing. These days, with students cramming for the endless exams they need to pass under No Child Left Behind, inane classes such as this are not as likely to occur; progress of sorts, I guess. But when I was in high school, such situations were not pleasant.

I remember a few other less-than-wonderful experiences in classrooms or other academic situations in high school because I couldn't hear what was going on, I wasn't sure how to deal with the situation, or I became tired of asking people to repeat themselves. In the early 1960s, before the Vietnam War turned off a lot of people, including me, to the military, our high school had something that was called either the National Defense Cadet Corps (NDCC) or the Junior Reserve Officers

Training Corps (JROTC). It was never clear to me if the official name of the program was NDCC or JROTC, but most of us called it "rot-c" anyway. All sophomore boys were required to participate in this program, and because the requirements were very clear-cut and the exams were directly from the manuals, I did quite well. We also had marching practice, usually outside, and the cadets, as we were called, frequently sang traditional military cadences during the drills. Not surprisingly, I couldn't understand most of the words. Should I have asked someone? Probably, but I didn't see that as particularly cool, at least in that macho setting, and simply said nothing as I tried to march in cadence with my classmates. I was able to take a driver's training course about five months into the school year instead of continuing my military education, and I never did learn the words to the cadences (although I did learn another skill, a skill which I haven't used too often since then: taking apart and putting back together a military rifle while blindfolded).

There are two other situations in high school worth mentioning where my hearing loss made it more difficult for me to participate in a way that I would have liked. I tried taking French one year, a rather traumatic experience that lasted about a week. Although I'm sure that there was some pedagogical purpose to the teacher's approach, as I recall it the class basically consisted of students calling out French words and phrases in response to the teacher's questions. Needless to say, for a hard of hearing student, this was not the ideal learning situation. Students were called on by name—from a seating chart most likely—to respond to the questions, and even though I had told the teacher I was hard of hearing and couldn't understand all the words, I was nevertheless occasionally called on to contribute an appropriate French word or phrase. I still recall the rather strange look from the teacher after I said something in French that, I'm sure, had absolutely no relationship to the way it was supposed to sound. I soon dropped the class, but this was yet another example of people, in this case an enthusiastic young teacher, not really knowing or understanding what the phrase "hard of hearing" meant. Or, if the teacher knew what it meant, it didn't really register and nothing much actually changed. Over the years, this has been a constant: telling people I was hard of hearing, that they need to talk more clearly, or louder, or face me, and then, after about thirty seconds, have them act as if nothing at all had changed.

A final classroom example comes from an English class on November 22, 1963, the day President Kennedy was assassinated. One thing I could hear, at least more often than not, were the announcements on the public address system, and I did hear the initial announcement that he had been shot in Dallas. I also recall that the teacher didn't appear to be too upset, something that characterized another teacher, later in the day, when he complained that school was being closed and students were told to go home after it was confirmed that Kennedy had died. I was quite upset, especially since I had seen JFK from a short distance only a few months before when he visited Salt Lake to deliver a speech. I had ridden my motor scooter to a part of town where he was riding in his limousine with the top down, probably one of the last times a U.S. president ever did that.

There was another problem for me in that English class: The instructor's teaching method was to call on students all the time, by name, and then check off the student's name when a contribution was made. This made for a lot of conversation in the classroom that was often difficult for me to follow. It also made me reluctant to contribute much, since I didn't want to repeat what someone else had said and, well, it was just easier to sit there and not make a fool of myself.

So much for some of my least enjoyable classroom experiences. How about dealing with the other, less structured situations outside the classroom? Even as early as elementary school I recall going to assemblies, listening to someone give a talk or make a presentation, and having a question or two. Invariably, I hesitated to ask a question because I thought that perhaps someone had already asked it or that the speaker had already talked about the topic. I had enough experiences where I did ask a question that had already been asked and answered that I hesitated to embarrass myself again. However, there were also times when, after a talk or presentation, I wondered to a friend what a speaker might have thought about a particular topic and the friend asked me why I hadn't asked the question when I had a chance.

What about parties, dances, and other situations where loud music, dim lights, and conversations that did not typically begin with people raising their hands and patiently waiting for someone else to finish were the order of the night? One solution was to simply avoid such situations. Clearly, there is no way that kids in middle school or high school, then or now, are going to raise their hands and take turns while talking at a party or a dance, nor is the music likely to get quieter anytime soon. However, there are things I wish I had done differently and which might have made my adolescent years less frustrating and more enjoyable.

Searching for Solutions

Looking back, it clearly would have been better for me or my parents to have made it more obvious from the beginning that I was hard of hearing and that we fully expected the school to accommodate my needs. This is much easier to do today than it was in the 1950s. Parents today, armed with the requirements of Public Law 94-142, can and should insist in their individualized education plan (IEP) meetings with school personnel that appropriate accommodations and services be provided for their child. Although schools are often reluctant to spend money they say they don't have on services they say aren't necessary, it is particularly important for parents—or other advocates for the child—to work cooperatively to ensure that the child's needs are met. More than a few parents have had to get the legal system involved in their efforts, but this should not be their first option, especially because any resentment that results from this process is likely to be felt first by the child.

In the late 1950s, when I was in the seventh grade, my mother wrote a note (shown here) on my report card that I returned to my homeroom

First Term of the _2nd_ Semester *Betty B. Christousen*

Parent's Signature

Parent Comments _TO ALL JOHN's TEACHERS_

We would appreciate any special consideration you can give John because of his hearing deficiency. He misses much of the class recitation.

A note on my report card from my mother to my seventh-grade teachers.

teacher. I have no idea if all my teachers saw this note, but there is no doubt that my mother wanted them to be aware of the situation and to give me some unspecified "special consideration." I don't know if there was any follow-up to this note or exactly what my teachers might have done (other than put me in the front row). However, because there were few if any legal mandates at the time, we were pretty much at the mercy of whatever goodwill the school system was willing to extend. This is in marked contrast to the situation today, in which parents and others have much more clout when dealing with recalcitrant schools and school systems to secure the services that are appropriate for their child.

I didn't have hearing aids when I was a child, so there was little outward indication to my friends and peers that I was hard of hearing. (I got my first one when I was nineteen; while I was growing up, my doctor said an aid would not be very useful for the high-frequency sensorineural hearing loss I had.) I must have asked them to repeat things, and there is no doubt that I simply missed many comments on the baseball field, the basketball court, and elsewhere, but I'm also sure that my status as a hard of hearing friend was not something that was as obvious to them as it could have been. Should I have made it more obvious? If so, how?

It is easy to say now that it should have been made clear to my friends and neighbors that I needed them to speak louder and more clearly, that I needed to see their lips when they talked, not to try to whisper in my ear, and so on. I'm sure that occasionally someone did tell them these things, but this didn't happen very often and didn't create much of a lasting impression. They probably had a hard time believing this because my speech was, and is, very good. Someone who didn't know I was hard of hearing would not be likely to figure this out simply by listening to me talk.

Having both good speech and a hearing loss creates an ambiguous or puzzling situation for other people. In the final analysis, it is not a bad thing to have good speech, but when I don't respond appropriately to someone's comments or questions, the fact that I didn't hear the person is typically not the first thing that comes to mind. Often it might be something like, "What's with this guy—is he a bit slow, or what?" People might not say this, but facial expressions and the rephrasing of comments or questions into simpler language usually give it away. Or, at least, that is how I sometimes interpret the encounter. It becomes another example of the looking-glass self: I am what I think you think I am.

How to handle this type of situation? One time as a teenager I was sitting in a youth meeting in our church and a lady behind me whispered something in my ear. For many people this would simply be a routine situation of no consequence, but for me it turned into another episode of tension city since I couldn't understand her and wasn't sure what to do next. Should I stop and say I was hard of hearing and that we needed to go into another room to talk? Looking back on this situation fifty or so years later leads me to say that that is exactly what I should have done. For some reason, this didn't seem like a good idea at the time, especially in front of my adolescent peers. No doubt I sat there for a while, dwelling on what my next move should be while trying to hear what the others in the group were saying. Later, after the youth meeting was over, I sought out the woman to say that I couldn't hear what she had whispered in my ear and to ask her to repeat it. This was long before I got a hearing aid, but because we were then in a fairly quiet area I had no trouble understanding her. (As I recall, it was an unimportant message to call my parents.)

In my case, my life would probably have been less complicated if I had simply started using a hearing aid earlier. Even if I didn't derive much benefit from the device, nevertheless it would have been fairly obvious that something was different about me and that it might be a good idea to talk loudly and more clearly.* Given my current status as a cochlear implant user and my experiences with that (which I'll discuss in more detail in chapter II), this assessment is probably overly optimistic. But at least it would have been better than taking the relatively small steps that my family and I took. On the other hand, I don't recall seeing another kid with a hearing aid while I was growing up. What would it have been like being the only child or adolescent in school with a hearing aid?

In sum, I may be naïve, but I think it would be easier today to make it obvious to friends and peers that a child is hard of hearing, and all that implies, than it was fifty years ago. For one thing, hearing aids are more ubiquitous today than they used to be; they are also smaller, more useful, and often less conspicuous. From the perspective of pure vanity, although they are not yet quite the same as having glasses and it is still unusual to see a child with a hearing aid in many schools, they

---

*However, at least based on my experience, many people seem to think that a hearing aid corrects a hearing loss the way glasses typically correct a vision problem. This seldom occurs. Although glasses may restore one's eyesight to 20/20 vision, hearing aids seldom restore one's hearing to "20/20 hearing." Thus, if people assume that by wearing a hearing aid the user can now hear well, this is *not* likely to cause them to speak loudly and more clearly. This is another ambiguous situation that those of us who use hearing aids, or even cochlear implants, have to deal with.

are no doubt more socially acceptable—that is, less stigmatized—than they were when I was younger (for which we can thank, at least in part, hearing aid users Ronald Reagan and Bill Clinton). In addition, we can thank legislation such as Public Law 94-142 (now IDEA), which has led to changes in behavior and attitudes that can be seen in schools and classrooms across the country. Cochlear implants, real-time captioning, classroom amplification systems, teacher aides, and professional sign language interpreters (as well as oral interpreters) are other options that parents of hard of hearing and deaf children have today that were either not available or not easily procured when I was growing up.

Leaving Utah

I left Salt Lake City in 1964 to attend Carroll College (now University), a relatively small, Presbyterian college in Waukesha, Wisconsin, about fifteen miles west of Milwaukee. I knew I wanted to go to a small college, where communication issues would presumably be more manageable than they would be in a large university, and I also wanted to leave Utah. Not only were many of my experiences as a hard of hearing adolescent somewhat unsatisfying, it was also not easy growing up as a non-Mormon in Salt Lake, particularly as the eldest son of my devout Presbyterian parents. My parents had both attended Wheaton College, an evangelical Christian college in Illinois, where, among other things, dancing was a distinct no-no. Unfortunately for me, dancing was a distinct yes-yes in Salt Lake, and I recall attending dances and other social activities as early as elementary school. There was always a latent conflict between what was expected of me socially and what my parents might have preferred, and I never resolved this satisfactorily while I lived at home. (My brother Dave, perhaps because he was the second child, did a much better job of ignoring our parents than I did.) There was always the unstated warning that I should not get too close to any Mormon girls or attend social events at Mormon wards (churches). Perhaps my parents were afraid that I would be tempted to convert; the Mormons actually try very hard to convert "gentiles" (non-Mormons) to their faith, and some of my friends became Mormon missionaries. In fact, in high school I was actually given a copy of the *Book of Mormon* by some friends as a Christmas present. My parents were not pleased.

Although I did occasionally break my parents' taboo by attending social events at Mormon churches (there were gyms at many of these wards and I sometimes played basketball there), I do not recall dating any Mormon girls while I was growing up. The dating pool for me was primarily limited to girls from our church or other Protestant churches in the area; this was not a large group, although it was a good one. At least going to a Presbyterian college would presumably change things in that regard, I thought. In addition, Carroll College was a college that had been attended by some of my cousins and was little more than an hour's drive from the ramshack in Cedar Grove, where my grandparents still lived, so it would be easy to get away for a weekend or for Thanksgiving vacation.

I worked as a delivery boy for a florist and on a building construction crew for about two months in Salt Lake after graduating from high school. After I had enough of that, I spent some time in Wisconsin with my family and relatives, enjoying my last few weeks of freedom before hitting the books in September. I also had my first serious romantic relationship. Beth and her family lived about two miles north of the ramshack, where they had a summer home on Lake Michigan. I don't recall how we met, but we had a great time that summer going to movies, walking on the beach, and doing the other things that young people in similar situations like to do. Communication was not really an issue with us, because Beth spoke very clearly and was soon aware that I was hard of hearing. This didn't bother her in the least. Her parents were easy to talk with too, even if we hardly ever agreed on political and social issues (they were very strong Republicans, at least at the time). While our relationship lasted, off and on, for a couple of years, it wasn't always easy to keep it going. Beth was still in high school when we started dating, and her parents were not too enthusiastic about her dating a college guy. Also, even though we were less than an hour apart, I didn't have a car, and the public transportation system between Waukesha and the suburban community north of Milwaukee where Beth and her family lived most of the year was pretty awful in the mid-1960s.

A little later, a few months after my freshman year of college when I got my first hearing aid, I called Beth on the phone from a store in Milwaukee. During our conversation, I mentioned that I had just gotten some new equipment, and she immediately guessed that it was a hearing aid (and thought it was a good thing that I had gotten one). The positive and supportive reaction from this future nurse gave me confidence that I could deal more openly and productively with hearing-related communication issues. It certainly helped me realize that there was no reason to feel embarrassed or self-conscious about wearing an aid. Much later, long after our relationship was over and we had our own families, my daughter Amanda became good summer friends with Beth's two daughters during our periodic vacations in Wisconsin.

During my freshman year at college, I enrolled in fairly small classes, which is what I expected in a small school. I still didn't have a hearing aid, but because most of the classes were lectures and I sat near the front, I had no trouble getting decent grades in my courses. I had initially planned to major in business administration but soon decided that I liked geography much better; the fact that my geography professor had a booming voice helped, too. I did have more of a problem in an English class, however, where there was much more classroom discussion. As usual, I sat in the front row, and there was a row or two of seats behind me. Although I could hear and understand the professor just fine, I could not readily understand what the students behind me were saying (and no one, including me, thought to put the movable chairs in a circle or semicircle so that everyone could see each other). I mentioned this to the professor in his office one day, and I recall that I was surprised to discover that he was surprised that I couldn't hear many of my fellow students. I guess I had unconsciously assumed that everyone was in the same predicament. He suggested that I think about getting a hearing aid; perhaps this is one of the reasons I decided to explore the hearing aid option again a few months later.

Another possible reason for initiating this exploration was that many outside-the-classroom activities proved to be no more enjoyable for me in college than they had been in high school. Wisconsin, as everyone knows, is the dairy capital of the nation; it is also the beer and bratwurst capital. I ended up pledging a local fraternity in my freshman year, and parties with plenty of beer were the order of the day. Late-night bull sessions were, too. In both situations, it was becoming even more obvious than it had been in high school that I was missing more conversation than I wanted.

One thing I clearly missed were the lyrics to the music that everyone was listening to in the midsixties, from the Beatles to Elvis to Peter, Paul, and Mary. The college cafeteria had music on virtually every day at lunch, but I couldn't make out many of the words. Some friends actually offered to write out the lyrics of various songs for me, but this was not something that happened on a regular basis. I pretty much just accepted this as the natural order of things, like I was used to doing in high school, but I was getting closer to doing something about it.

I got my first hearing aid in summer 1965, between my freshman and sophomore years of college. I was working as a handyman that summer at a small family compound on a lake near Pewaukee, Wisconsin, about a half-hour drive from Waukesha. I needed to return to Utah during the summer for some surgery and, while there, decided that it might be a good time to get a hearing aid. The ear, nose, and throat doctor who I had been seeing for years told me that some new aids had come out recently that might work well for me since they could be adjusted to amplify high-frequency sounds, which is what I needed. Unfortunately, we didn't think about the possibility of having the vocational rehabilitation office pay for the device, and my parents covered the cost. Fortunately, it wasn't too expensive, although it represented a significant chunk of my father's ministerial salary.

The aid didn't made a great deal of difference during the first few months that I wore it (on my right ear only). I could make out higher frequency sounds, such as birds chirping and people whistling, that I couldn't hear very well (or at all) before, but other than that there was not much change. I still couldn't understand the words in the music that was played in the cafeteria or at parties, it was still difficult to communicate in noisy situations, and I could use the telephone just fine with my left ear. Very soft conversations, such as whispering, were still impossible, as were conversations in situations where it was difficult to lipread. This made for some awkward dating situations, but because I was not inclined to advertise my hearing loss other than my visible hearing aid, I didn't give the matter a lot of thought. I didn't notice much difference in the classroom either. Some of my friends thought I was hearing better with the aid, but if so it was a very minor improvement.

The Philippines

During my sophomore year, I decided to either transfer to another college or go abroad for my junior year. Carroll College participated in a junior year abroad program sponsored by the Presbyterian church, and as the 1965–66 academic year progressed I decided to try to get into that program. There were a number of colleges and universities around the world that were involved in this program, and I needed to decide which one I might like to attend. Because I didn't speak a foreign language, it would have to be at a university where English was the language of instruction. I considered the American University of Beirut and the International Christian University in Tokyo; English was used in both places. I finally decided on Silliman University in the Philippines, primarily because my cousin attended Carroll College several years before, went to Silliman during her junior year, and had a wonderful time. Over the years, I had talked with her about her experiences and had seen her photographs. For a lack of any compelling reason to pick another college, I decided to go there.

In summer 1966, I flew from Salt Lake to San Francisco for a few days of orientation with three students from other Presbyterian colleges who were also going to the Philippines for their junior year. Two of them went to the University of the Philippines, near Manila, and one of them joined me at Silliman, in Dumaguete City, about four hundred miles south of Manila.

My experience in the Philippines was life-changing in many ways, and international travel and living has been an important part of my life, and the life of my family, in the years since then. For one thing, Filipinos are incredibly friendly folks, and some of the friendships I developed there were among the closest I've ever had. However, it took me a bit of time to become comfortable with some of the norms, or rules for behavior (such as a completely different definition of personal space

With friends on the Silliman University campus.

My dorm bed (the top bunk) at Silliman University,
complete with mosquito net.

than is found in the United States, where touch is often not something
that happens right off the bat). Some of the food took a while for me
to get used to, and some of the accents were more difficult to understand than I expected, even with my relatively new hearing aid. I never
got used to eating rice at every meal, the daily afternoon siestas, or the
pleasure of an invigorating cold shower at seven o'clock in the morning.

There were still plenty of ambiguous and difficult listening situations
in the Philippines, but the professors at Silliman were generally easy to
understand (some of them were Americans), and I had no difficulty in
my classes. Among other things, there was almost no class discussion;

Filipino students rarely asked questions or made comments in class. The lecture method, for all its faults, was used almost exclusively, and it was easy to follow. In fact, in one class the professor basically read his entire lecture word for word each day. This was incredibly boring, but because we were expected to copy everything he said, it left little room for misunderstanding.

One ambiguous listening situation happened fairly early in my experience in Dumaguete City. I had brought an inexpensive Polaroid camera with me and was walking around the community taking some photographs. I was in a very poor area of the city and soon attracted a crowd of dozens of young children, each of whom wanted me to take their picture. There was no way I could take a photo of each kid, and, as far as I could tell, none of them spoke English, so it was difficult to tell them this. If I had taken one child's picture, then I would have been overwhelmed with demands from the others that I take their picture, too. I don't recall how I extricated myself from this situation, but I probably took one or two group photos, gave the instant black-and-white Polaroid prints to one of the kids, and waved goodbye.

The fact that I had a hearing aid was something that didn't come up very often in the Philippines. The most obvious difference between me and most Filipinos was my height, not my hearing status; I was much taller (something that I had in common with some of the other Americans, male and female, on campus). This seemed to generate more comments in my everyday encounters with friends and acquaintances than my hearing loss or the fact that I wore a hearing aid.

One problem with a hearing aid in the Philippines, however, was that in a hot and humid climate there were inevitable technical problems. I was unaware of the havoc that such a climate plays on sensitive electronic equipment such as hearing aids or cameras and didn't take appropriate precautions. After a few months, my aid stopped working.

There was no place to send it for repairs in the Philippines, so I had to send it home. Those were the days long before overnight delivery companies like FedEx were in business, so it was weeks before I got the aid back. While my aid was in the United States, I simply did without. Even though I had been using the device for only a little over a year, I clearly noticed the difference. During the time I didn't have a hearing aid, my junior year abroad companion and I took a trip over Christmas break around Mindanao, a large island in the southern part of the Philippines. There were inevitable communication problems on this trip. Because I didn't have a visible hearing aid on my ear, if I didn't take the time to explain why I couldn't understand what people were saying it was easy for them to conclude that I was unfriendly, "stuck up" or worse. Consequently, I was delighted to have my aid waiting for me when we returned to campus in Dumaguete City in early January.

One of the highlights of that trip was a visit to a rubber plantation located near the Pulangi River in the central part of Mindanao. We had to take a six-hour ride on a motorized *banca* (a type of outrigger commonly used in the Philippines), followed by a hike of several miles, to reach the isolated plantation. After spending an exhausting day there learning things about rubber trees that I've long since forgotten, we boarded a hastily constructed raft about ten o'clock that night to take us back down the river. I described this raft and the trip in a letter I wrote to my family after getting back to Silliman:

> This was really some raft. It was made out of bamboo and some logs which were to be used as firewood. We didn't get back down until seven the next morning. There is nothing like trying to sleep with my head on one sack of corn, my butt on another sack, and my feet spread out over a low spot of the raft which was completely under water.

I slept, although I woke up suddenly as we were going through a particularly rough spot on the river with a massive cliff right in front of us. Fortunately, the guy standing behind me at the back of the raft had done this before and skillfully steered the contraption around the

The raft on the Pulangi River, December 1966.

rocks. I must have been drenched, and it was a good thing that I didn't have a hearing aid to protect while trying to keep my balance on my far-from-first-class seat.

Living without a hearing aid for a few months while mine was being repaired gave me an early taste of how I was slowly but surely becoming more dependent on technology. Of course, the type of technology available in the 1960s is exponentially different from what we have come to take for granted. The relatively simple hearing aid I had then has little in common with the sophisticated, programmable digital devices available today. Another form of technology that has changed dramatically since then is the telephone. When I lived in the Philippines, international telephone calls were prohibitively expensive, and I didn't have any phone contact with my parents or anyone else during the entire time I was living abroad. Even a three-minute call would have cost more than $100. Mail service was incredibly slow as well. This made the distance between the United States and the Philippines seem even greater than it was. Contrast this with the experiences we had when our daughter Amanda was teaching English in Japan forty years later and when our son Andy was living in London about the same time. Both of them had their Macs with them, and we had one at home, so frequent and free video chats were the order of the day. Our oldest child, Erik, also taught English in Japan several years before Amanda, and before video chats had become common, but international phone calls were a lot cheaper than they were in the 1960s. In general, video chats have been a godsend for deaf and hard of hearing people, enabling us to talk, sign, and lipread with ease even over thousands of miles.

―――

One of the most rewarding experiences I had in the Philippines was playing baseball for the Silliman University team. As I mentioned, I was quite involved with baseball as a kid and even played a little at Carroll College before going to Silliman. I played center field on the team, batted cleanup (fourth in the batting order), and traveled to a number of different cities for games, including a tournament with the University of the Philippines in Manila. We happened to be a very good team, even in our old, mismatched uniforms, and defeated the University of the Philippines squad and many other teams from around the country. As can be seen from the photo, there were several other Americans on the team (primarily from missionary families—Silliman University has a long history of being supported by, even founded by, American missionaries), and we had a fabulous pitcher from the Mariana Islands who should have been pitching for the Yankees.

―――

Silliman baseball team; I'm third from the right in the back row
(not the guy in the sunglasses).

One day early in 1967, I was studying in one of the libraries at Silliman and noticed a beautiful Filipino woman walk into the room. I asked one of my friends, "Who is that?" I hadn't noticed her before, even though our paths had apparently crossed a few times. I don't recall how we got started talking, but we were soon doing things together and, if we had had more time, perhaps the relationship would have developed into something more permanent. As it happened, my American junior year abroad companion and I had made plans to leave Silliman in April, a week or two before the semester ended. I wanted to travel around the world on the way home, and she needed to get back home for her wedding. Consequently, I had only a few weeks to get to know Pearl, the young woman I noticed in the library. During this time, I quickly realized she was a special person. In addition to being idealistic and extremely hard working (as people who wake up at four o'clock in the morning tend to be), she felt very strongly about her religious beliefs and was devoted to pursuing a life of service. I learned a great deal from her and look back fondly on the short time we spent together.

For some reason, Pearl had to be in Manila on the day I left the Philippines, and we had planned to say goodbye at the airport. Unfortunately, there was a massive traffic jam on the route to the airport, and I only had time to say hi and goodbye to Pearl before boarding the plane. We kept up a correspondence for more than a year, but in the end the distance was too great and the circumstances too complicated for our relationship to continue.

This was in 1967. Amazingly enough, I was able to get in touch with Pearl again in 2002, this time thanks to Google. Sometime in late 2001 or early 2002, I read a newspaper article about doing a "Google search" to find people, something I had not heard about before. I thought about some people I had known in the past and wondered if it would be possible to find them using this method. Somewhere along the line, I searched for Pearl. I knew she was married but had no idea what her married name was. However, I remembered her surname, as well as her real first name (Perla), so I typed that to see what would come up. After reading through some of the search results, I noticed the name of someone with her first name, her maiden name, and a new last name. There was also an address in the general Manila area with the Philippine Department of Education associated with the name. There was no e-mail address or even a complete street address, but I decided to write a short air-mail letter, which included my e-mail address, to see if she was the person whose name appeared on my screen.

Several weeks later, I received an e-mail from someone whose username and address I did not recognize. As I started reading, I still had no idea who was writing, since I had pretty much forgotten about my note and the writer didn't identify herself until late in the e-mail (and was using someone else's account). I was surprised to discover that it was Pearl, but not surprised, given the drive and ambition I remembered that she had back in 1967, to learn she had an important position in the Philippine Education Department. After a few more e-mail exchanges, she mentioned that she would be in San Francisco in a few months for an international reading conference, and we arranged for her to fly to

Washington to meet Arlene and our children, all of whom happened to be in the D.C. area when she was here. Pearl spent almost a week with us and, among other things, met a lot of people at Gallaudet. This relationship bore fruit a few years later when one of my favorite students, a Filipino by birth, went to the Philippines and had a remarkable and rewarding internship under Pearl's supervision. Thanks to e-mail, it has been easy to keep in touch with Pearl from time to time in the Philippines, where she continues her life of work and service, especially in what is called *whole-brain literacy* (which the reader can easily find more about by doing a Google search).

Back in the USA

After I left the Philippines in April 1967, I spent about two months traveling west through Hong Kong, Thailand, India, Iran, Iraq, several other countries in the Middle East, and Europe. I don't recall a lot of major communication issues on this trip, probably because my hearing aid was in good working order. In any event, if I didn't know the language and if others I encountered didn't know English, then my hearing loss was not much of an issue anyway. I traveled very cheaply and stayed at a lot of youth hostels and other inexpensive digs along the way. (It was a major hassle to contact my parents and ask them to send more money—this was long before automatic teller machines, Visa, and MasterCard.) I stayed in an old Salvation Army building in Calcutta (now Kolkata), a YMCA hotel in New Delhi, and, in Cairo, found a place that cost about 25 cents for the night. When I went to sleep, the large dormitory-style room with a dozen or so beds was completely empty; when I woke up in the morning, it was completely full. It was nice to sleep through what must have been a fairly noisy situation, but it was also a bit disconcerting. Outside of Cairo, I climbed up to the top of one of the great pyramids (on an inside stairway, not on the outside), and in Beirut I attended a Pete Seeger concert. En route from Jordan to Israel, I must have been almost the last American to pass through the old Mandelbaum gate before the Six-Day War began a few days later (by which time I was safely in Greece).

------*mm*------

After returning to Carroll College for my senior year in fall 1967, I was faced with the problem of deciding what I wanted to do when I grew up. I had taken a lot of sociology and religion courses at Silliman and thought about going to seminary. My father was still a minister, and while I was in the Philippines my family had moved from Salt Lake to Kenosha, Wisconsin, about a hour drive from college. My father's parents, who were in their nineties and still living at the ramshack, were in good health, and this was one of the main reasons my parents decided to leave Utah. I also thought about the Peace Corps. I ended up applying and getting into Union Theological Seminary in New York City, a well-known liberal Protestant theological seminary. I had become quite interested in liberal theology in the Philippines, reading such theologians and philosophers as Reinhold Neibuhr, Dietrich Bonhoeffer, Viktor Frankl, and Erich Fromm, and I thought that I might like to pursue some of the issues they examined in more depth in graduate school. I really couldn't see myself as a traditional church minister, partly because of my hearing loss and partly because I wasn't sure exactly what I believed. Whatever my religious beliefs were at the time, they were pretty far removed from what I had learned in Sunday school. I also came back from the Philippines with a heightened social conscience and wanted to do something to "change the world," or at least some part of it. Such idealism was not unusual among those of us who graduated from college in the tumultuous year of 1968. Martin Luther King Jr. was assassinated a month before I graduated, and Robert Kennedy was killed two months later (and, interestingly enough, Eugene McCarthy, an antiwar Democratic candidate for president in 1968 and a candidate in the important Wisconsin primary, gave a campaign address at Carroll College at the very moment that President Lyndon Johnson announced he would not seek reelection).

—*mm*—

By fall 1967, the Vietnam War had become something that college-age males could not avoid thinking about. Like many of my contemporaries, I had not thought too much about the war in Southeast Asia before heading to the Philippines in mid-1966. If I had any sentiments at all, they were probably more along the line of "we need to do what needs to be done to stop Communism from spreading" and "we need to support the president and the troops." However, after living for a few months in the Philippines; talking with friends and acquaintances about the war, colonialism, and related issues; and reading more about the history of Vietnam, the Philippines, and Southeast Asia, I came to see things quite differently. By the time I returned to the United States the following summer, I was very opposed to the war.

At the time, the United States had a military draft, but males enrolled in college enjoyed a student deferment until they graduated or reached the age of twenty-four. Because I was hard of hearing, I was assured by my doctor and by audiologists that I would not be drafted, but I was still nervous and thought that the military might try to find a way to put me in uniform. I had friends who ended up in 'Nam, and I wasn't at all interested in joining them.

In March 1968, about two months before I was scheduled to graduate from college, I participated in a week-long volunteer stint with several of my classmates in Biloxi, Mississippi. I don't recall much about what we did there during our spring break, other than to work and play with some young children, sleep on the concrete floor of a church in sleeping bags, paint, and play touch football on the beach (a welcome contrast from the cold in Wisconsin). One thing I do remember is that I talked to my father on the phone during the week, and he mentioned that I had gotten a letter from the Selective Service System, the government agency responsible for the military draft. Because I would soon be leaving college, I had been ordered to take the dreaded physical exam in a few weeks.

Even though I knew in my head that I would fail the physical, I was still very anxious when I got the news. In fact, I was nervous the whole way back to Wisconsin, a trip that took even longer because our car broke down and we had to spend several days in Tennessee waiting for repairs.

The physical exam took place in April, and the young men from the Waukesha area were bused to Milwaukee at some ungodly early hour. Fortunately for me, I didn't sleep through my alarm; I hate to even think of what the consequences might have been for not showing up for my Army physical. The ride was about an hour to the location where we had the exam. The mood in the bus was pretty somber, and I'm sure most of the guys on the bus fully expected to pass the exam; I was nervously optimistic that I would fail.

For those who have had an Army physical exam, it is without question a never-to-be-forgotten experience. Hundreds of anxious males in groups of fifty or so moved from one venue to another, filled out impossible-to-understand forms, provided urine samples (or at least tried), spread buttocks for the most intimate of inspections, and took the inevitable hearing test. As one might surmise, communication difficulties appeared early and often in this acoustically challenging environment.

Soon after we arrived at the facility, I was seated in a large room and asked to fill out a form. There was a small blank box on it, and my group was told to write in some letters and numbers that, as far as I could tell, had no obvious meaning; they were just arbitrary numbers and letters. I was sitting some distance from the person who was talking and couldn't hear what we were told to write in the space. What was I supposed to do? Raise my hand and say I couldn't understand the instructions? Stand up and complain? Perhaps this is what I should have done. However, things were moving along quickly, and I needed to write something. Consequently, I simply turned around and copied what the person behind me had written. I told the guy that I couldn't hear what the man (a sergeant, perhaps) giving the instructions was saying and asked him what the numbers and letters meant. My seatmate said he had no idea, and that he just wrote down what he was told. Not having any better idea at the time, I simply wrote down the same thing.

Sometime after filling out the form, our group ended up in a part of the building where they tested our hearing. I had the foresight to bring a letter from my ear, nose, and throat specialist in Salt Lake with me, as well as a letter from another expert, attesting to the fact that I had a hearing loss and that I would be of no value to the military. I didn't expect the person administering the test to read the letters and send me home without testing me himself, but I figured that having some ammunition, so to speak, wouldn't hurt. In any case, I was eventually sent into the testing room and asked to respond, by pushing a small button, to pure tones given at different decibel (loudness) levels and at different frequencies.

Sometimes when taking such a test a deaf or hard of hearing person is not sure exactly what is heard, whether it is something imagined or if it is an actual sound from the testing device. This is why the tester must frequently backtrack, going over the tones again and again, to determine the threshold between hearing and not hearing. Sometimes, at least for me, this can lead to some awkward periods of silence, when one just sits there, wondering if the tones are actually coming through, or whether they are there but cannot be heard, or whether the audiologist has given up and gone to lunch. I felt this awkwardness in the hearing test during my Army physical. After going through the lower frequencies, which I could hear, the audiologist moved on to the higher frequencies, which I could not hear. I just sat there for several minutes, doing nothing. After it was all over, the person administering the test gave me the printed audiogram, which showed, as I expected, a steep downward slope from left to right on the graph: a good deal of hearing in the lower frequencies but virtually nothing in the higher frequencies. This was similar to many audiograms I had had over the years. I thought to myself that this is good news indeed and should keep me out of the Army. Unfortunately, these results, coupled with the letters, were still not enough, and they made me do the entire test again. Maybe they were surprised, but I certainly wasn't, that results of the second test were exact duplicates of the results of the first one. Because there was now irrefutable evidence that I couldn't hear well enough to serve in the military, I was classified as 4-F, which meant that I would not be drafted and did not need to retake the physical exam in the future.

My mood on the bus back to Waukesha after the physical was quite different from the mood of the others. As far as I could tell, I was about the only one who had successfully failed the exam. I was elated and, with graduation approaching, could start thinking about other things far removed from the military.

Chicago and Arlene

Shortly before graduating from college, I was accepted into the Peace Corps and went through part of the training program that summer. After several weeks, however, I decided that the program they had assigned to me, teaching math to elementary school kids, was not something I wanted to do for the next two years. After I started the training program, I had told Union Seminary that I would not be coming after all, and when I left the training it was too late for them to find a place for me. Fortunately, I was able to get into McCormick Theological Seminary in Chicago, the same seminary my father had attended. They came up with a significant financial package at the last minute, so I thought to myself, why not? There didn't seem to be anything else very promising on the horizon, and I didn't have to worry about the draft. (Even if I had been eligible for the draft, being a student in a theological school or seminary would have meant a deferment; I'm sure this was the reason some of my male classmates were there.)

Hearing issues cropped up from time to time during seminary, mostly in ways similar to those in college. Like in college, the ambiguous and uncomfortable situations in which I sometimes found myself often led to feelings of inadequacy and confusion. One weekend I attended a party in a noisy and crowded room and tried to talk with an attractive girl who was also apparently interested in talking with me. I was with a friend who knew that I was hard of hearing, and to his credit he tried to help me out as much as he could. However, it was just too loud, and after responding inappropriately to some of her comments, she obviously lost interest. What should I have done? Not going to the party in the first place would probably have been the easiest choice. Perhaps I could have suggested that we step outside and chat; unfortunately, this was in the middle of winter in Chicago, so if I had suggested that she probably would have thought I was nuts. Years later, when I first read David Myers's *A Quiet World*, the following sentence brought back memories of situations like this: "To be hard of hearing is sometimes to look and feel like a fool."

In a different situation, another friend (my roommate actually, a friend from college) and I were in a noisy bar in the Windy City with two other guys we knew from college. Again, it was impossible to hear them and to participate in the discussion. I was dependent on my roommate for a ride, so I had a few bad choices: I could just sit there and nod my head and smile, get up and walk around, find something to read, make comments from time to time that had nothing to do with the conversation, ask them to repeat what they were saying, try to find a place to lie down for a nap, and so on. Or I could have suggested that we leave the bar and find someplace quiet. This didn't occur to me at the time, however, and even if it had, I suspect that they would not have been interested in doing it. As with other situations like this, I tolerated the situation as best I could, tried not to show that I was angry, bored, or irritated, and waited it out.

Over the years, I have been faced with many similar situations, and solutions to the communication problems inherent in such settings are not much easier to find today than they were forty years ago. If there is a standard solution to this problem, I suppose my basic strategy is to try to avoid such situations as much as possible. Certainly I try to avoid noisy places, socialize with people I know well, and, if possible, interact with others who sign. In this, I have been somewhat successful, although it is impossible to avoid all stressful listening situations. Moreover, the vast majority of hearing people I come in contact with do not know how to sign.

—*um*—

As it happened, I did not enjoy seminary very much and soon began to scout around for something else. McCormick was located very close to DePaul University, and I eventually found my way to DePaul's placement office, looking through brochures for various postcollege programs. One program that caught my eye was a Masters of Arts in Teaching program offered through Antioch College in Ohio. The program was called the Antioch-Putney Graduate School of Education and was located in the Germantown section of Philadelphia. Antioch College is a very progressive, even radical, institution, and the program offered applicants a chance to take relatively unstructured courses, as well as teach with pay, so the cost would presumably be manageable. I had thought about teaching social studies in high school even before leaving for the Philippines, so perhaps this was exactly the kind of program that would work for me.

Two good things came out of my experience at seminary in Chicago. One was learning about the Antioch-Putney program, which eventually led to my career as a sociologist, and the other was meeting my wife, Arlene, at a singles group at Fourth Presbyterian Church, an imposing Gothic revival structure right across the street from the John Hancock building on Michigan Avenue.

As my short-lived seminary experience was winding down, several of the guys and I decided to go to this singles group and check out the scene. I have no idea how we found out about the group; perhaps there were some notices posted somewhere or perhaps someone had circulated a flyer. In any case, having nothing better to do on a Sunday evening when the group got together, we decided to go. I was very unimpressed and saw little reason to go again, but a week or two later we decided to try once more. This time I saw someone in the back of the room and said to myself, "Who is that?" I didn't see anyone that attractive the first time I was there. I eventually made my way to where she was standing with some friends, and we started talking. Fortunately for me, it was quiet enough that I could hear her just fine (thank God for heavy carpeting, furniture, and curtains in these old, comfortably endowed churches), and we had a good conversation. We were both back the next week (she later admitted that she had noticed me across the room, too), and we started dating. At first, I was a bit apprehensive about asking Arlene out. She is an outgoing, vivacious extrovert, and I tend to be somewhat more reserved. At least part of my introversion is because I've learned to be leery of "saying something stupid," especially when I'm in a challenging communication situation. Over the years, Arlene has encouraged me with at least some success to be more outgoing in encounters with others. As I will describe later, since I started using a cochlear implant in 2001 I have had more success in this regard than I did when I was using one or two (or no) hearing aids.

—◆—

Our first date was to see the movie *Charley* on a cold spring evening, and we quickly began seeing each other on a regular basis.* Arlene had just started teaching elementary school music in suburban Chicago the previous fall. She had a car, which made it easy for us to get together. She was living at home with her family in Park Ridge, where she had

---

*Interestingly enough, I don't remember if I could hear the dialog in this film very well. Perhaps I wasn't paying too much attention. Some of the other films of the era, such as *A Man for All Seasons*, were impossible for me to understand, and I remember sitting through this long film, understanding almost nothing, and hoping that it would end quickly. I occasionally saw action-packed James Bond films, as well as subtitled foreign films at the Biograph Theater in Chicago (made famous as the place where the gangster John Dillinger met his maker), and these were much better.

spent most of her childhood and adolescence (along with her Park Ridge high school classmate, Hillary Clinton).

Shortly after we began dating, I received an acceptance letter from Antioch-Putney and decided to move to Philadelphia; there was no point in trying to stay in seminary, and there were no other decent educational options on the horizon. At about the same time, Arlene's father was transferred to Denver, and she told me that she was thinking about applying to a graduate program in education at Colorado State University in Fort Collins. Because we had been dating for only a few months, we had to figure out what to do. One option would be for me to go east and for her to go west while somehow trying to keep things going. As this was long before the Internet, cell phones, and inexpensive air travel, this was really no option at all. Or, I could forgo Philly or she could forgo the possibility of Fort Collins, and we could continue dating in a new environment. In the end, we actually chose Plan C, which at the time seemed incredibly hasty but over the years has worn very well. We decided to get married that summer. This was 1969, before the sexual revolution had made much headway, and living together was not something we thought about. Even if we had, our parents would have been both appalled and totally opposed to it. Also, because these were the days before the most recent chapter in the women's movement really got off the ground, there was little doubt that we would end up in Philadelphia after our wedding. In fact, Arlene easily got a teaching job in one of the suburban communities outside the city.

After we decided to get married, we rushed to make the arrangements for the ceremony, which took place in late July in Arlene's church in Chicago. Because my family was now living in Kenosha, Wisconsin, just an hour or so north, it was easy to arrange for my father to officiate. I worked at a department store in Kenosha selling men's clothing for much of the summer and kept the Illinois Tollway in business by driving back and forth to Park Ridge as often as I could. After the wedding and a short honeymoon in Mackinac Island, Michigan (borrowing a car from my father and some money from my brother), we pulled a small U-Haul trailer attached to Arlene's Volkswagon bug to Philadelphia.

—*mm*—

Communication issues were not paramount during the time Arlene and I were dating. We were not in a lot of noisy situations where it was difficult for me to hear (we didn't go to many noisy bars and rock concerts), and she had no issues with the fact that I wore a hearing aid. In fact, the matron of honor at our wedding, a lifelong friend, was a teacher of deaf students in New Jersey. I had a relatively new in-the-ear hearing aid, and even if I did sometimes miss what people said, asking them to repeat it was more than enough to get by. At the time, I still had no problem conversing on the phone.

My parents, though, were concerned that I might have difficulty understanding Arlene. They had been somewhat overprotective of me, and they were concerned that she talked too fast and that I wouldn't be able to consistently understand her. I assured them that this was not a problem. My father, being a conscientious pastor, was also concerned that we were getting married too quickly and that we did not know each other well enough. Consequently, he wanted us to take a paper and pencil test that he frequently gave to couples before their marriage. After taking the test, which included questions about finances, goals for the marriage, what happens if something goes wrong and so on, the couple would sit down with my father and discuss their differences. Presumably this type of counseling would be helpful for the newlyweds, especially during the first few years. We thought the test was a bit unnecessary, but because my father was pretty persistent and probably hoped that it might slow down our rush to the altar, we answered the questions separately. After my father compared the results, he was quite shocked to discover that we had the highest level of compatibility he had ever seen. After that, he pretty much kept his own counsel.

Soon after we arrived in Philadelphia in August, Arlene began teaching elementary school music again and I started the master's program at Antioch-Putney. After not having to think much about communication issues for several months, they became important again soon after I started the new program.

Communication Norms

An important part of the educational experience at Antioch-Putney was a paid teaching position, typically in a public school in Philadelphia since the program was primarily designed to prepare people to teach in urban public education, either at the elementary, middle, or secondary levels. To teach in such situations, aspirants needed to take a variety of educational courses to become certified (as they still do today). One of the things that attracted me to the Antioch-Putney program was that these courses were very flexible, and one could satisfy the requirements by studying topics and issues that one might not find in a more traditional educational setting.

Many of the classes I took in the Antioch-Putney program were quite unstructured, and a lot of them involved a great deal of informal class discussion. It was often difficult for me to participate in these classes, especially because my classmates did not typically raise their hands and wait until someone else was finished talking before offering their observations. These were not situations I could easily walk away from since they were part of the curriculum. Many people in the program probably knew or had some vague awareness that I was hard of hearing, but I suspect there was a general lack of understanding about what that meant and what one was supposed to do about it. These were not insensitive people. Even though these were the days before issues related to disability and disability rights became salient, they were people who were extremely concerned about the war in Vietnam, racism, and other issues that were part of the political and social landscape in the late 1960s and early 1970s.

—*mm*—

There is a dearth of social explanations for communication difficulties faced by many deaf and hard of hearing people, especially when trying to communicate and interact with hearing folks. Sure, it is important for a deaf or hard of hearing person to remind others to speak clearly and distinctly, not to use exaggerated mouth movements, and so on, but there is a shared responsibility too. There is also the problem of acoustics and the inevitable importance of cultural norms. Although much can be done to make it easier for deaf and hard of hearing people to hear and/or communicate in a particular setting (adding a lot of fabric to the walls, floors, and windows, for example, as well as having good lighting and a minimum of glare), the frequently unstated and unexamined norms need to be taken into account as well. Questions such as the following need to be addressed: What are the implicit or explicit rules for communication in a particular setting? Are people expected to take turns, or is it expected that people will simply jump in and talk (or sign) when they feel they have something to say? If they talk, should it be a soft whisper, a conversational voice, or a loud shout? If they sign, should they use their voice while signing? How does the setting itself play a role, whether it is a formal church service, for example, or a family dinner? How rigid are the norms: can they be easily violated with no consequence or will be one escorted out of the room if a particular standard of behavior is violated? Questions like these are literally endless, but they remind us that most of the norms that we take for granted are quite arbitrary. Once we become aware of how arbitrary they are, they become more amenable to change. The question then becomes, What is the best way to change some of them to make communication easier, as well as more productive and satisfying?

In retrospect, I'm sure that many of the classes I took in the Antioch-Putney program would have been much more enjoyable for me if I had been more open about my hearing loss, if I had made it clear from the beginning that I was missing a lot of the conversation, and if I had insisted that things needed to change if I was to have an opportunity to participate in the discussions. Perhaps I could have specifically suggested that people agree to take turns while talking, that the discussion leader be responsible for enforcing this agreement, and that people make an extra effort to speak up. I don't know if this would have made any difference, but at least it would have made me feel that I had done what I could. After all, since I was paying tuition, I should have received the same benefits from the program as anyone else—an argument that in retrospect is obvious but didn't occur to me at the time.

The communication norms or rules in these relatively informal class settings were not very rigid, and consequently it might have been relatively easy and painless for everyone to have modified some of them. While this, too, might seem obvious forty years later, it is still difficult for me to do this in practice, especially in a group of a dozen or more people or with people I may not know well. It is often easier and less disruptive to try to muddle through and focus on things over which I have more control. As I will discuss later, the assistance of an ally in an effort to deal with uncomfortable and challenging communication situations such as this, especially by changing some of the implicit communication norms, is something that could be very useful for a deaf or hard of hearing person. Moreover, now that we have laws such as the Americans with Disabilities Act (ADA) and IDEA on the books, there is a legal responsibility for educational programs such as the one in which I was participating to make sure that students with disabilities have access, including communication access, to their programs.

In the final analysis, many hard of hearing people, especially those who experience a loss of hearing later in life, are frequently reluctant to say much about their hearing loss, and many of them do not even bother to get their hearing tested or wear a hearing aid. This, too, reflects our norms: In spite of what people sometimes say, and in spite of the fact that Presidents Reagan and Clinton both used hearing aids while in office, having an aid is still not the same thing as wearing glasses. In spite of efforts to miniaturize hearing aids and make them virtually invisible, having a hearing aid carries more baggage than wearing glasses. Consider, for example, the press coverage in the 1990s when President Clinton got small, inside-the-ear hearing aids. There was considerably more ink spilled on that story than on the nonexistent story that he also needed reading glasses.

One of the unintended consequences of wireless communication technology, where people sometimes use a Bluetooth headset that looks very much like a behind-the-ear hearing aid, may be that it will become increasingly common to see a piece of technology on or near one's ear in the future. As this becomes more common, it could easily lead to a reduction in any feelings of shame or embarrassment that hearing aid or cochlear implant users might feel. Indeed, I was at a large warehouse store recently and had to look twice at the equipment that was attached to one person's ear to see if it was a cochlear implant, a hearing aid, or a wireless telephone device. Whatever it was, it didn't look very different from the cochlear implant I was wearing.

Becoming a Sociologist in Pennsylvania and Wisconsin

Late in the fall of 1969, those of us in the Antioch-Putney program were supposed to start looking for somewhere to teach the following spring, and like my classmates I had to be medically certified by the Philadelphia school system to teach in the classroom. As part of this assessment, I had to have a hearing test, and for some strange reason the school system's medical officer insisted on giving me the test sans hearing aid. Since I would obviously use the aid in class, what was the point of giving me a hearing test without it? Neither I nor the people I was working with at Antioch-Putney could understand this, but we did not challenge the school system's decision in any systematic way. Today, such discrimination would be inconceivable. The end result was that I was unable to teach in a Philadelphia public school. Because I was still in the program, I was faced with the need to find someplace else to teach. As it happened, this was an incredible bit of luck.

For some reason, one of my classmates was not assigned to teach in the public school system, and I learned that he would be teaching sociology at a community college in downtown Philadelphia instead. I had taken a number of sociology courses in college, especially in the Philippines, but had not thought much about pursuing sociology as a field of study. Since I would not be teaching in the public school system, I wondered if it might be possible for me to do the same thing my classmate was planning to do, either in Philadelphia or somewhere nearby.

After observing a number of community college classes in Philadelphia and in Bucks County, a few miles north of the city, I ended up teaching several introductory sociology courses at Bucks County Community College in Newtown, Pennsylvania, from January to August 1970. I had to prepare like mad for these courses, since the only thing I knew about sociology was what I had learned as an undergraduate student, but the experience was quite rewarding. I was reasonably good at it, and most important, discovered that I really enjoyed studying sociology and wanted to pursue more education in the field. Unfortunately, I realized this after most of the deadlines for getting into a graduate program in sociology for the fall semester had already passed.

I managed to get accepted into a master's level program in sociology at the University of Wisconsin, Milwaukee (UWM), secure a teaching assistantship, and even get in-state tuition, all in the late spring and early summer of 1970. Fortunately, I had not changed my voting registration or my driver's license from Wisconsin to Pennsylvania, and this may have made it easier for me to get into UWM; at least it enabled me to avoid costly out-of-state tuition. In any case, it was the beginning of my career in sociology, and in August Arlene and I made the trip back to the Midwest and settled down in Milwaukee. Again, Arlene had no problem securing another teaching position, this time in a school system just north of the city.

I was a student at UWM from 1970 to 1972, where I got my first real exposure to academic sociology. I had a great deal of catching up to do, especially in areas of social theory and research methodology, and spent a lot of time in independent study courses during the first semester. Many of my other classes were quite large, and I often had difficulty following the discussion, even though I sat near the instructor whenever I could. Perhaps as a consequence of this, I decided early on to focus primarily on writing rather than talking. That is, I spent a lot of time writing the papers that were typically required in each class rather than worry too much about what I said in class. I figured that the professors were more likely to put a lot more emphasis on an actual product, be it a paper or a take-home final exam, than on "class participation." This turned out to be a very good decision.

I had some very good mentors at UWM, many of whom had gotten their doctorates at the University of Wisconsin, in Madison, or at the University of Chicago, two of the top-ranked sociology departments in the country. As I became more knowledgeable about sociology and worked with some of them as a teaching assistant, they encouraged me to pursue a PhD in the field, which I eventually did.

―――

After I graduated with a master's degree in sociology from UWM in May 1972, I taught for a year at one of the two-year campuses of the University of Wisconsin, in Janesville. Most of the communication issues in the classes I taught were fairly minor, and I managed to muddle through with occasional guesswork and bluffing and by asking students to repeat (sometimes more than once) what they had said. If worse came to worse, after class or before the next class, I tried to find those students whose comments I couldn't hear to ask them what they had said. (Asking students to remember what they had said in class a couple of days earlier is not a strategy I would recommend, however.)

...and in California

In the fall of 1973, I began a PhD program in sociology at the University of California, Riverside (UCR). In contrast to many of my classes at UWM, at UCR most of the graduate courses were quite small, and many of the other graduate students and faculty members were aware of my hearing loss. Consequently, I participated much more in the classes and seminars there than I had at UWM, but I still put much more time and energy into my written work which, again, was a smart thing to do.

I got to know several UCR faculty and graduate students quite well, and a few have remained longtime friends. Even here, when communication issues came up, it sometimes proved difficult to know how to respond. I remember being in one small seminar and my hearing aid started to give off a some annoying whistling or feedback, presumably because of an ill-fitting ear mold. I couldn't hear it, but the professor asked, "Does someone have a hearing aid?" I didn't feel comfortable saying that I had one; I simply fumbled with the knob and turned it down so the whistling went away. I knew the professor, who wasn't much older than I was, but he apparently didn't know I had a hearing loss. (The early to mid-1970s were the days when many men, including me, let their hair grow quite long, and it was easy, intentionally or not, to hide a hearing aid.) I also knew most of my classmates in the small seminar. Nevertheless, it was still difficult for me to say anything, and, in retrospect, I'm embarrassed that I was not more forthcoming. Another time, a class met outside for one of the sessions, and I had a terrible time understanding what was going on. Again, I didn't feel right interrupting the professor or my fellow students to ask that we find another place for the class. In this case, I told the professor after class that I couldn't hear what people were saying outside and that is why I didn't participate very much that day. As I recall, that was the only time this class met outside.

I asked Morrison (Morri) Wong, who has been a friend since our graduate school days at UCR and who has been a professor of sociology at Texas Christian University for more than thirty years, if he had any recollections of communication difficulties during our years at Riverside. He said that when I was using my hearing aid, communication difficulties were not very noticeable to him but that when we were playing tennis (and I wasn't using the aid), some creative signs were necessary. He wrote in an e-mail to me:

When we played tennis together (actually against each other), you were just a person I competed against. However, there were things that I may have done to better communicate with you on the court. Instead of saying, 'Nice shot, John,' not knowing whether you heard it or not, I gave you the finger. In fact, I probably gave you the finger quite a few times during the set. It was my way of making sure that you knew you made a nice shot. . . . There were a few times that you and I played doubles together against sociology faculty. I did notice that when you and I teamed up, when I praised you for a shot, you didn't turn around to acknowledge the praise. It was at these times that I remember saying to myself, 'John is hard of hearing.' So what I would do is wait until you turned around, say 'nice shot' so that you could see my lips, and then pump my fist or raise my thumb.

―――

In addition to my work in graduate school, Arlene and I had our first child while we lived in Riverside. Erik was born in April 1974, about six months after I started the PhD program at UCR. As it happened, I was able to be in the delivery room when Arlene gave birth, although it was not something that was routinely offered to fathers in the mid-1970s. I had to sit behind Arlene so I would be out of the way (which made it a little awkward for me to assist her with the breathing exercises we had learned in our Lamaze class) and was sternly told to "sit down" when I stood up to see things a bit more clearly. In any event, there wasn't much communication with me in the delivery room, and since I didn't know any sign language there was no interpreter present (and I suspect that it would have been a hassle to have requested one even if I had known how to sign at the time). Three years later, when our second son, Andy, was born in San Luis Obispo, there was no question that I would be in the delivery room and assist Arlene, although communication was still somewhat of an issue because I still didn't sign and the face masks worn by the doctors and nurses obviously made it impossible for me to lipread. By the time our daughter Amanda was born in Washington, D.C., in 1981, I knew how to sign and we were easily able to arrange for a sign language interpreter to be present in the birthing room (all night, in fact). Moreover, I was offered the opportunity to cut the umbilical cord after Amanda's birth, something that had not happened for either of the two boys. It was an offer I was more than delighted to accept.

What about Gallaudet?

While at Riverside, I had my hearing aid serviced from time to time, and I also got an occasional hearing test to see how my hearing loss was progressing. I also decided to try to learn more about the cause of my hearing problem. I had been told as a child that my loss was due to "nerve deafness" and, a few years earlier, had even tried to determine whether surgery might be helpful. I had a friend in Milwaukee who had surgery to correct a conductive hearing loss. After looking at my audiogram, her surgeon informed me that surgery would not be appropriate in my case. Later, while living in Riverside, I explored the issue further since it was becoming increasingly difficult for me to understand students in class and, consequently, to teach the kind of class I wanted to teach. It was much easier for me to do most of the talking, and, because I liked using simulation games, group discussion, films, videos, and other nontraditional methods, there was an increasing dissonance between the image I had of myself as a professor and what I actually ended up doing in many of my classes. I could try to resolve the dissonance by either changing my pedagogy or by changing my image of myself as an instructor. If I continued to do most of the talking and had a more teacher-centered classroom, then I would no doubt eventually come to see myself as a fairly traditional, lecture-oriented professor. I didn't want to see myself this way, however, and didn't want students to perceive me this way either, so it was necessary to find a way to incorporate more discussion and interaction into the classroom. Having a progressive hearing loss made it increasingly difficult to do this.

In this context, I made an appointment at an audiology center in Redlands, California, not too far from Riverside. This was late in my graduate career, and I had already started looking for a job. In fact, I may have already had some interviews at the time of my appointment. Although it had been possible to work around the issue in graduate school and part-time positions, when it came to a traditional tenure-track job the issue of my hearing loss was going to be a big deal. Two interviews that I had for teaching positions in the Midwest demonstrated this. In a group interview, I had to ask people frequently to repeat their questions. Finally, one person asked me straight out whether I had a hearing problem. I said yes and explained that I told my students about it on the first day of class. I told the students that if I asked them to repeat something it wasn't because I was ignoring them or because I wasn't paying attention to their question, but simply because I couldn't hear them. This usually got a few chuckles from the students and helped to create a more comfortable classroom environment early in the semester. Over the years, I had discovered that it was easier to ask students to repeat something they had said if the reason for asking them to do so was clear. In retrospect, it is amazing that it took me quite a while to realize this. However, after reading David Myers's account of his experiences in the classroom in *A Quiet World*, it appears that my tardiness and awkwardness in this regard was hardly unique. During the job interview, the obvious question was, if I did that in my classes, why didn't I say that to the group interviewing me? By this time, my hearing loss was more noticeable and it was becoming difficult to use the phone without amplification. In addition, because these job interviews were not very satisfying or ultimately very successful, I realized that it might be difficult to find the kind of job I wanted in a traditional academic setting.

This was about the time I ended up at the audiology clinic in Redlands. I hoped, in the back of my mind, that perhaps my hearing loss was correctable and that maybe I was doing things to aggravate the situation. (Blowing my nose too hard was something I actually thought about!) Or perhaps there were newer, more powerful hearing aids available that could make a difference. During the course of my visit to this center, one of the audiologists asked me what I was planning to do when I finished my dissertation. I said I was still looking for a job and that, so far, had not found anything. She asked me, "What about Gallaudet?" I had never heard of Gallaudet, and said, "What's that?" She said it was a college for deaf students in Washington, D.C., and that it might be worth exploring. I had actually visited the Pennsylvania School for the Deaf in Mt. Airy, a section of Philadelphia, when I was in the Antioch-Putney program, so I had a little exposure to younger deaf kids, but I didn't realize there was a college for deaf students as well. This was one of those "aha!" moments; Gallaudet, I thought, could be a great place for me.

The contrast between my visit to the Pennsylvania School for the Deaf in fall 1969 and my encounter with the audiologist in Redlands in early 1976 illustrates the importance of circumstances in defining such eureka moments. As mentioned earlier, I needed to find a place to teach in the Philadelphia area as part of the Antioch-Putney program. My visit to the Pennsylvania School for the Deaf was to see if I might want to work there. However, I didn't identify with the students, perhaps because I didn't sign, and consequently did not see this as a place where I might want to teach. I even remember that one of the kids excitedly pointed to my hearing aid and the teacher said that, yes, I had one, but I had only a mild hearing loss and therefore was not really "one of them." Seven years later, the communication-related frustrations I had experienced in the classroom, my own progressive hearing loss, and my desire to find a teaching position I might enjoy led to a far different reaction when I first learned about Gallaudet.

This was long before the Internet age, so I wrote a letter to "the president" of Gallaudet, saying that I was hard of hearing, completing graduate school, and wondering if they had any openings in either sociology or psychology. (I had a lot of coursework in social psychology and had taught courses in that field as well.) The president, Edward

Merrill, didn't respond to my letter, but John Schuchman, the dean of the college, wrote to say that they had just filled positions in both departments and didn't have anything at the time but would keep me in mind for the future. Well, I thought, it was worth a try, and I started to look for something else.

The something else turned out to be a one-year position at Cal Poly in San Luis Obispo, a medium-sized city located on the coast halfway between Los Angeles and San Francisco. One member of their faculty was taking a sabbatical leave during the 1976–77 academic year, and I filled in while he was gone. This was a very good experience, both for me and for my family. The central coast of California is a beautiful location, and I had a nice, supportive environment in which to finish my dissertation. I still had the typical communication issues in class, but they were not terrible and I was asked to consider staying.

—*mn*—

During this period, I had little contact with any type of sign language, and while at Cal Poly I even inquired about taking lipreading lessons so that I could understand the students better. (I was told that lipreading was more of an art than a science and consequently wasn't something that could easily be taught.) In general, though, if a student had a question or comment, if the others in class were reasonably quiet, and if the question or comment had something to do with the topic we were discussing, I could do alright. In any event, I don't recall any students complaining to me, to my various department chairs, or on the end-of-the-semester course evaluations that communication issues made it difficult for them to succeed. Faculty meetings were another story, as my colleagues did not tend to take turns while talking. I was pretty quiet in such settings, both because I was often unsure what people said and because I was very much the low man on the totem pole.

—*mn*—

In the middle of the year, I was contacted by the sociology department at Gallaudet; they had an opening for the following fall and said I was welcome to apply for the job. I was elated and planned a visit to the college regardless of whether they invited me for a formal interview. I had set up a trip during spring break to several colleges on the East Coast that had vacancies and replied that I would be coming to visit Gallaudet in March. As it happened, they invited me for an interview, and I spent a day and a half on campus.

Since I didn't have any other solid job prospects on the horizon in spring 1977, I was nervous about the interview at Gallaudet. I arrived the evening before, by train from Philadelphia, and took a cab to the campus. I found my way to the dorm, where I spent the night. I had never been around many deaf people before and was surprised to discover how noisy the dorm was.* In fact, the racket continued most of the night, and I got very little sleep before my interview the next day. The first person I met was Yerker Andersson, a Deaf man who was the chair of the department. I didn't know any signs, so he and I had to communicate by writing back and forth; lipreading didn't work for us either. After talking with Yerker, I met the other members of the department, which included both sociologists and social workers as well as the dean. There were a lot of one-on-one interviews, but I was not asked to do a class presentation. I did, though, observe one class and was delighted to see the free-flowing communication that took place there. I thought that this would be an ideal situation for me. During the discussion in this class, one of the students was not using his voice and the instructor (a hearing person) asked him to do so. The student

---

*In retrospect, one of my biggest regrets during my graduate school career in Riverside was not being more aware of the California School for the Deaf, one branch of which is located in Riverside, only a few miles from UCR. If I had known more about this school, the Deaf community, and issues related to sociology and deaf people earlier in my career, I might have had a very different graduate school experience. In particular, I'm sure my dissertation would have been quite different. However, for whatever reason, I was not ready for this experience in the early 1970s.

readily complied with the request. In the 1970s, the method of communication generally used at Gallaudet was Simultaneous Communication, or SimCom. This method emphasized speaking English (or mouthing the words as if speaking) and signing in English word order at the same time. This method continued for a number of years but gradually became supplanted by a "voice-off" policy that reflected the growing importance of ASL on campus. When using ASL, it is not possible to sign and speak at the same time because ASL and English have completely different grammatical structures. (ASL has French, rather than English, linguistic roots.)

Following my interview, I flew back to California and was picked up at the Santa Barbara airport by a very pregnant Arlene and our three-year-old son Erik. As we drove north to San Luis Obispo, I told them about the interview and how excited I was about Gallaudet and the possibility of teaching there. I didn't know if they would offer me a job, but by the time we got home, we all hoped that things would work out so that we could move to the nation's capital.

At Gallaudet, they had told me when they would be making their decision, and I anxiously waited for the phone to ring in my office at Cal Poly a few weeks later. I remember that I was getting ready to go to a class that day when the phone rang. Dick Meisegeier, one of the sociologists on the faculty, was on the line, and he offered me the job. (Fortunately, I had asked the people at Cal Poly for an amplifier for the handset on the telephone in my office, so I could hear him reasonably well.) I was naïve about salary and benefit negotiations and immediately accepted, even before I had any idea what the job paid!

I had about two months left at Cal Poly before we had to leave for Washington so I could participate in an eight-week sign language program. During that time, we had our second child (Andy), sold our house by ourselves in about twenty minutes (I'm not kidding) in the red-hot coastal California housing market, and drove a rental truck to D.C. with the four of us crowded together on the front seat for much of the trip.

I tried to teach myself a few signs and some fingerspelling before we got to Washington and spent hours that summer in class and in the evening trying to learn how to sign as quickly as possible. Those were the days before sign language videos were readily available for home viewing, so practice basically consisted of looking at simple drawings in a book of someone signing a word or concept and trying to copy the sign. The other new, nonsigning faculty and professional staff and I spent hours in class going through the book, learning and practicing new signs (using SimCom). It was important for those of us on the faculty to learn to sign quickly because we would have to sign for ourselves in all of our classes at the beginning of the fall semester. Unlike the situation at Gallaudet today, new signers at the time were not provided with an interpreter, even for one semester. It was a classic case of sink or swim. I'm sure many students were bored to death in my classes, at least during the first few months, and I, like all of my new signing colleagues, was faced with communication difficulties in class that were both embarrassing and nerve-wracking. In one class, I nervously tried to explain a sociological concept during my first semester, and one student told me, "You've got a long way to go." In a different class, a student pulled out a newspaper and started reading; I kicked him out of class. And contrary to my experience in the class observation during my interview, students often did not want to use their voice. As a consequence, it was sometimes very difficult for me to understand what they were trying to tell me, especially at the beginning. One of the reasons I was so excited about coming to Gallaudet in the first place was because of the perceived ease of communication in the classroom. It didn't take me long to realize that this was not something that was going to happen overnight.

Over time, as I became more immersed in my new life at Gallaudet, it became clear that I had made the right decision to come to Washington. I readily passed all of the sign language evaluations, enjoyed most of my classes, especially as I became a more fluent signer and could understand my students, started serving on faculty committees, and began doing some research related to sociology and deaf people. I also relished the easy collegiality and interaction with my faculty colleagues and others on campus; virtually everyone I encountered over the years on Kendall Green—as Gallaudet's campus is known—signed in my presence, and this made communication a breeze. It was wonderful to be in a place where a person with a hearing loss was perceived as being perfectly normal.

Two Worlds

Although communication with colleagues and students soon became a nonissue, outside of Gallaudet I primarily interacted with nonsigning hearing people and consequently faced many of the same problems that I had to deal with before. Over the years, these communication problems have not changed very much, although many of them became more manageable when I started using a cochlear implant (as I'll discuss later). Communication at home was not a big problem, especially since Arlene learned how to sign and fingerspell quite well, although I'm sure it could have been better. My biggest regret is that I didn't sign very much with my family. After signing all day, I was generally tired and everyone could readily understand me when I talked. Looking back, it would have been better if Erik, Andy, and Amanda had learned more signs (although they, along with Erik's wife Shanna, do sign occasionally and all fingerspell reasonably well). In addition, I should have made more of an effort to wear my hearing aid all the time at home and not force everyone to have to seek me out when they wanted to talk with me. We also could have taken more time around the dinner table to make sure that people took turns talking, that we didn't talk with our mouths full, and so on. Outside my immediate family, however, with hearing friends, extended family members, kids on the sports teams I occasionally coached, neighbors, and back-to-school nights and parent conferences, it was generally a different story, with many of the same types of communication difficulties that I had experienced as a child and as a young adult.

—*mm*—

Yes and No
by Amanda Christiansen

One of my favorite examples of our family's unique communication style is from my childhood, when I would have to call on my father to bring me something at school. When we were younger, he would sometimes work from home for some portion of the day, and I would be able to call our house if I'd forgotten something (which I always did) or if I needed to come home because of some childhood illness. Since our phone's ring was a fairly high-pitched sound that was difficult for my dad to hear, we had a light that would blink on and off when it rang. As these were the days before Caller ID, he was less than eager to answer, but if it was during school hours he was willing to take the plunge in case his kids needed him. That was the easy part. Our method for phone conversations was to limit it to "yes/no" questions only, as in he would ask a question and I would respond. However, "yes" and "no" sounded virtually the same to him on the phone since they are both one-syllable words. Consequently, I would respond either "Y-E-S" (three distinct sounds) or "N-O" (two). "Did you forget your lunch?" "N-O!" "Are you sick?" "N-O!" And so on, until we got to the right question and answer. Fortunately, there are not too many reasons why a child calls their parent while at school. Those two questions usually covered it. I'd get off the phone in the office of my elementary school feeling confident that my dad would come to the rescue and look around at confused faces of whoever may have been in the office. I'm sure I sounded pretty silly to those secretaries, teachers, the nurse, and others, but I felt that it was perfectly normal and that there was something wrong with them if they didn't understand. My father most likely felt frustration for not being able to communicate easily, but I felt special because we had our own secret (OK, not so secret) code. Unlike my dad, I've never been one to steer away from making a scene. In many ways, I have him to thank for that.

One of the problems I frequently encountered as a hearing aid user was not knowing if what I was able to hear was at all similar to what others were hearing (or what I thought others were hearing). Moreover, because I frequently experienced feedback or whistling while using my aids, I often wondered if this was occurring, especially in a quiet room, even when it was not. Sometimes it was not clear to me if people were reacting to something I said or something else that was happening in the surrounding environment. All this proved to be confusing and disconcerting and reinforced my reluctance to take the initiative and try to modify the situation.

On several occasions when speaking in front of a group of nonsigners, I was interrupted by someone because of communication problems that I was unaware of. In one situation, at a banquet for a youth basketball team I coached in the mid-1980s, I was making some comments when someone came up and told me to talk closer to the microphone. Although this type of thing happens to many people, including those without a hearing loss, it was yet another reminder that because it was not easy for me to monitor the sound of my own voice, especially in a large room, it was difficult to know how loudly or softly to speak or how close I should be to the microphone. These situations are more easily managed now that I'm using a cochlear implant, especially because I am able to hear higher frequency sounds that I was not able to hear with a hearing aid. Also, it is nice that there is no possibility of feedback or whistling when using an implant.

I coached several youth teams while my kids were growing up, and communication with the young players was not always easy, especially in a loud gym with several people talking or screaming at the same time. In addition, even when I was officially the coach, other adults were sometimes involved, and with several adults trying to tell the players what to do at the same time it doesn't take too much imagination to guess how difficult it was for me to hear and understand what people were trying to say. However, we made it through the games (which we even won occasionally), and we usually enjoyed ourselves by keeping things focused on the kids as much as possible. At least in basketball, it was easier to manage the communication situation by getting everyone to focus on the plays I diagramed on an erasable board. (Not that it did much good once the kids went back on the court, as everyone who has coached young athletes knows.)

—⁓—

In her book *Alone in the Mainstream*, Gina Oliva writes about two social worlds, the world of a vibrant Deaf community in which people share a common culture and communicate comfortably with one another in ASL and the more diffuse world of hearing people. She suggests that, given the choice, most deaf and hard of hearing people would likely want to be involved with both worlds. Others, too, have suggested that being a part of both worlds can be both rewarding and enriching. So it has been for me.

One area where being part of both worlds was particularly rewarding and enriching was at some of the professional meetings I attended, especially when another deaf person was there and we had the services of a sign language interpreter. In particular, I recall one meeting of the American Sociological Association in Toronto a few years after I started at Gallaudet. By that time I was a fairly fluent signer, and my Deaf colleague Yerker Andersson and I attended this meeting together. Not only did we benefit from the interpreters in the sessions, but we also had a nice time talking (signing) at restaurants and other locations outside of the formal meetings. In fact, Arlene and the kids were with us, and she complained that I was spending too much time with Yerker! But because it was easier to communicate with him than my nonsigning colleagues, especially in noisy settings, I ended up spending a lot of time with him.

Sign language interpreting at professional and academic meetings and conferences has been a mixed blessing for me, however, because the quality of interpreters varies quite a bit (especially outside of cities like Washington, D.C., or Rochester, New York, that have large Deaf communities), and some of the technical material is difficult to interpret in any case, especially if the interpreter is not familiar with the vocabulary. I recall attending a conference on George Orwell in, not surprisingly, 1984, and having a terrible time trying to understand what the speakers were saying because the quality of interpretation was so uneven. Today, more than a quarter-century later, with the availability of PowerPoint and real-time captioning as well as higher quality professional interpreter training programs, communication difficulties such as this are much less likely to occur.

Although being part of both the loosely defined hearing world and the more cohesive Deaf world has certainly been enriching for me, in some ways it has been a rather strange and sometimes difficult juxtaposition. If one imagines the Deaf community at one end of a football field and the hearing world at the other, I'm pretty much on the fifty-yard line. But I'm not just standing and relaxing at midfield; I'm exhausted from running from one end of the field to the other, and I'm trying to catch my breath before starting to run again.

This was pretty much what my life was like while I was at Gallaudet. In many ways, especially before I got my cochlear implant, it was a very unequal world, with the ease of communication and the respect I received from students and colleagues at Gallaudet for my work there in contrast to the frequent isolating and embarrassing experiences I had with many hearing people at other times of the day. Given that, why don't I spend most of my time in the Deaf community? Why spend so much time in the hearing world, where being unable to hear well is frequently a time-consuming hassle and a nuisance? Part of the answer is that this is all I knew for the first three decades of my life, and, for better or for worse, that is what I became comfortable with. Moreover, that is the world of my family as well as most of the people I see on a daily basis, even more so now that I am no longer teaching at Gallaudet. It is also easier for me to interact with those in the hearing world than it used to be because I now have a cochlear implant. However, Gallaudet and the Deaf community are important parts of my life, too, and in one way or another, that will continue to be the case in the years to come.

An Ambiguous Status

I mentioned earlier that the phrase "hard of hearing" is quite vague and includes those who have a mild hearing loss as well as those who are very hard of hearing. A hard of hearing person frequently occupies a marginal or in-between position that can easily result in a disconnect between how the hard of hearing person sees himself or herself and how others see the person. A major issue is how to manage this problem; it is a big job and one that requires constant monitoring.

Sociologists suggest that any status or position plays an important role in the way a person perceives the world. A person's position as a father, for example, obviously influences the way he sees the world, as does a person's position as a mother, a teenager, or a recovered alcoholic. Moreover, others tend to use statuses as shorthand ways of classifying a person and act accordingly.

Although there are a number of statuses that sociologists talk about, one that has particular relevance here is something called "master status." Basically, this is the most important or primary position that one has. A master status can be something that a person has achieved through individual effort, such as college professor or drug dealer, or something that is ascribed (that is, acquired or inherited) without effort, such as being female or being a deaf person. A person's master status plays a dominant role in that person's life, even if it changes from time to time. For example, at one point in a person's life the status of college student may be the most important position. At another point, this may not be important or even relevant.

I would venture to guess that for many hard of hearing people, the fact that one is hard of hearing is typically *not* that person's master status. In other words, other positions, such as mother, son, daughter, lover, plumber, pediatrician, and so on are likely to be what is most important to the person. On the other hand, for many Deaf people, being a culturally Deaf person *is* often a master status. While I was teaching at Gallaudet, we often discussed this issue in some of my classes, and many students did select being a Deaf person as their master status. Many did not, but we also discussed the likely possibility that if we were doing the same exercise in a typical hearing university, no one would select the status of hearing person as their master status. Being a "different" or "nonstandard" member of society no doubt heightens one's sensitivity to that particular attribute and consequently makes it more important. Like many other minorities, one is forced to think about one's status on almost a full-time basis; hearing white males usually don't need to do this.

Even though I suggest that a hard of hearing person would typically not select that status as a master status, the problem is that other people—that is, hearing people—may be inclined to do so. A hard of hearing person may be an accomplished athlete, a father, or a business executive, but in encounters with others what frequently comes to the fore is not the accomplishment but the fact that the person has a hearing loss. At the very least, this is annoying and can lead to feelings of resentment and even anger. Of course, this can and no doubt does happen to deaf people, as well as to other people who are members of a minority group. A deaf PhD might define herself as a PhD first, but others might be more inclined to see the deafness part as being more important. An African American doctor or a Hispanic lawyer might be inclined to see their accomplishment as their most important position, but others might be more likely to focus on their racial or ethnic status.

An Ambiguous Situation

In this chapter, I have described a number of situations that have reinforced my in-between status as a hard of hearing person. This is something that many other hard of hearing people have commented on, implicitly or explicitly, in writing or in person. Being neither hearing nor deaf means, among other things, that one may not be fully a part of either world. This often leads to confusion, both in terms of one's identity and in terms of how one should act in various situations. There are frequently no clear norms about how hard of hearing people are supposed to behave in situations in which they find themselves, especially when interacting with hearing people. Equally important, there are often no clear norms about how hearing people should behave vis-à-vis hard of hearing people (or deaf people, either). Ambiguous situations like this can cause anxiety and frustration; they certainly have for me. Given this state of affairs, both for me as well as for many other deaf and hard of hearing people, what insights might sociology offer that could help explain why this happens, as well as what might be done about it?

Perhaps ironically, in an ambiguous situation where there is an absence of clearly understood norms, it may be easier for a deaf or hard of hearing person to take the initiative and try to redefine or restructure the situation to make it more comfortable and productive for all concerned. In addition, at least in my experience, many hearing people I come in contact with do want to do the "right thing," even if they have no idea what that might be.

In ambiguous situations, people may be amenable to suggestions, especially from someone who is willing to take the initiative or who may be in a position of authority. Social science research, especially classic social psychological research conducted by the late Yale psychologist Stanley Milgram, suggests that sometimes this power or influence can have undesirable consequences.[8] In these experiments, naïve "teachers" were told by the person running the experiment (who was typically dressed in an authority-reinforcing white lab coat) to administer an "electric shock" to a "student" each time the latter made an error on a simple word-pair test. Although the shocks were fake, as were the screams by the student—who was not a student at all but someone working with the experimenter—many teachers went along when the experimenter and administered what they thought were actual electrical shocks to the error-prone student. These experiments are especially noteworthy because the perceived voltage increased each time the hapless student made an error. In the end, many (although not all) of the teachers in these experiments followed the directives of the experimenter to the extent that this could have resulted in the student's death had they been actual shocks.

Another example is the Stanford prison experiment. This experiment was conducted by Philip Zimbardo and his colleagues in summer 1971, when a simulated prison was created in the basement of one of the buildings on the campus of Stanford University. In this experiment, twenty-four male students were randomly selected to be either a nebulously defined "prisoner" or a "guard." It was initially expected that this role-playing experiment would continue for about two weeks, but before the first week was up the experiment was terminated because, as Zimbardo wrote: "In less than a week the experience of imprisonment undid (temporarily) a lifetime of learning. . . . There were dramatic changes in their [both the prisoners' and the guards'] behavior, thinking and feeling. . . . We were horrified because we saw some boys (guards) treat others as if they were despicable animals . . . while other boys (prisoners) became servile, dehumanized robots who thought only of escape."[9]

Although in this ambiguous situation ordinary people—especially the "guards"—generally behaved badly (as did the "teachers" in the previous experiment), there are other situations where the norms are not clearly defined that can have positive outcomes. For example, a hearing person may come in contact with a deaf or hard of hearing person for the first time and have no idea what to do, what to say, or how to say it. In ambiguous situations such as this, the person who is willing to take the initiative and define the situation in such a way as to promote a more positive outcome is likely to have some influence. In such situations, the responsibility would typically fall on the shoulders of the deaf or hard of hearing person, even though this might be difficult to do. As I've mentioned throughout this book, this has been difficult for me to do over the years.

The phrase *definition of the situation* is one that sociologists have used for decades to emphasize that the meaning a situation or an act has for people is not something that exists apart from how it is defined. Polygamy, for example, can be defined as either acceptable or not acceptable, depending on how people in a particular society (or a powerful segment of society) see it. Some types of behavior, such as incest, are so universally condemned that there is little cultural variation among definitions; the incest taboo applies everywhere. For many situations, however, there is considerable ambiguity, and this opens up opportunities for people to try to influence or define how people should or should not act. I will offer some thoughts about resolving communication difficulties after mentioning a few additional communication-related issues as well as a few embarrassing words about bluffing.

Bluffing and Other Communication Stories

In *A Quiet World*, psychology professor David Myers, who has a progressive hearing loss, writes about how difficult and nerve-wracking it was for him in the classroom, when students occasionally snickered if he answered a question inappropriately or misunderstood a student's name, or at home, when he misunderstood what his wife or his children were trying to tell him, or when he said something inappropriate to friends or colleagues that did not fit the general topic being discussed. In such situations of failed communication, it seems natural to assume that the problem is with the person who, while attempting to fit in and be a part of the group, ends up saying something stupid and making everyone nervous or embarrassed. Myers, like Henry Kisor, who wrote about his experiences as a profoundly deaf person in his book *What's That Pig Outdoors?*, suggests that the failure is almost entirely his fault, and that if any improvements are to be made they need to be done by him, not by anyone else. As Myers notes, for him there were a lot of "bad hear days."

While it may be admirable, and probably very American as well, to appropriate a "pull yourself up by your own bootstraps" mentality, it is both short-sighted and counterproductive to put the blame only on oneself or on one's hearing loss for the communication difficulties deaf and hard of hearing people frequently face. Certainly, if a person with a hearing loss wants to communicate with people who have "normal" hearing, certain commonsense steps are warranted: a hearing aid, if appropriate, perhaps a cochlear implant, a quiet, well-lighted room with good acoustics, and so on. It is also important that bluffing, that is, pretending to understand a conversation when you really don't, be eliminated or at least minimized. Over the years, I have been involved in more situations than I care to remember where I have not understood what someone was saying and continued to nod my head or in some other way tried to assure the person I was talking with that I understood what he or she was saying, even when I didn't. Perhaps one reason for doing this is because I tend to become anxious and frustrated in such situations, and I'm frequently not sure how to try to manage them. This is particularly likely to happen when I realize that asking someone to repeat a comment or question is not likely to do much good anyway. Unfortunately, ill-advised nodding often leads to embarrassment when it becomes obvious that I am not following the conversation. Sometimes other people become angry that I have wasted their time (and, by pretending, that I have devalued their comments), and they certainly have a legitimate reason for their anger. Often, after the encounter is over, I feel some anger and disappointment as well, usually directed at myself for being unwilling or unable to take the initiative and do something to make it easier for us to communicate. Or, if conditions are such that it is simply impossible to communicate, to say so and try to make arrangements to talk at another time and place.

Situations like this are a recurrent problem faced by many hard of hearing people, and many of us continue to struggle to come up with a workable solution. Perhaps the best strategy is to make it clear at the outset that you are deaf or hard of hearing, that you look forward to having a good conversation, and that you want to work together to make sure that happens. No doubt this is easier said than done, especially in a large group or with people you don't know very well. But if things such as this are done, and other people still don't take a few simple steps to make it more likely that clear communication will take place, or if they say something like "never mind, it's not that important," or "I'll tell you later," then it is silly for a deaf or hard of hearing person to feel guilty, feel a sense of shame or anxiety, or blame themselves if communication breaks down. However, that seems to be what often happens.

David Myers writes: "I do not blame those who utter these words [never mind], which sometimes are accompanied by a shake of the head, rolled eyes, or a dismissive gesture. What else should people do? What would I do in their place?"[10] Although Myers may not blame other people, I would be inclined to do so, especially because such comments are basically the mirror image of bluffing: If I'm not taking the other person seriously when I pretend to hear when I don't, they are not taking me seriously when they brush me off and refuse to take a moment to repeat what they said or to work cooperatively to find another way for us to communicate.

Part of the problem is that many hearing people simply do not know what it is like to not be able to hear well (or at all). Sure, they may see their elderly grandmother having trouble hearing the television or talking on the phone or the kid down the block who signs and talks funny, but for the most part they don't have much contact with people like that, and it's easier to ignore the whole thing and focus on more immediate concerns. Most people simply do not have that much to do with people who are different, whether they are of a different race, a different religion, or a different set of physical attributes. As a famous (unknown) amateur sociologist once said, "birds of a feather flock together."

One of the consequences of a general lack of contact between people with a hearing loss and those with "normal" hearing is that when they actually meet, there are few guidelines about how to behave. The norms in such encounters are vague and of little practical guidance. As far as they go, they often lead to discomfort, confusion, and embarrassment. Consider, for example, David Myers's frequent feelings of anxiety and self-consciousness in front of his class. These are feelings that I have experienced as well, especially before I ended up at Gallaudet University.

As I mentioned before, I taught at several colleges and universities in Pennsylvania, Wisconsin, and California before coming to Washington, D.C., and more than thirty years after these experiences I still cringe at some of the awkward and even humiliating situations. One time at UCR, a student came up to me after a class to thank me for raising an issue in a class discussion that had some particular meaning for her. I didn't hear what she said at first because other students were mingling around and making some noise, and I asked her to repeat it. She said it again, and I still wasn't sure. Finally, I understood what she said (after quickly going through several possibilities in my mind), but it was awkward and I'm sure the student left with a feeling that there was something strange going on here and at the very least probably did not feel comfortable approaching me again. On another occasion, I had a conversation outside of class with one of the young professors at UCR. We were waiting in line for lunch, and I thought he said that he was from Chicago. I replied by saying my wife was from the Chicago area, too. He didn't say anything in response to that, and I didn't think much more about the conversation until months later when I found out that he was actually from New England. Looking back, he must obviously have wondered why I said what I said, apparently out of the blue, in response to his comment. If I had known there was a misunderstanding, I could have said something, but because I didn't and perhaps because he wasn't even aware I had a hearing loss, he probably started wondering what a doofus like me was doing in graduate school.

In retrospect, I should have made my hearing loss clear to the students at the beginning of each course. (I started doing this later; the student mentioned in the previous paragraph was in the first class I taught at UCR.) If I had stayed in a more traditional (i.e., non-Gallaudet) university setting, I'm sure I would have done that on a regular basis. Even so, some important questions remain: What difference would it really make? Do hearing students actually understand what it means to have a professor with a hearing loss? Would they do anything differently? My guess is that for most people this would be simply chalked up as a vaguely interesting tidbit and without frequent reminders would be typically ignored or forgotten.

Resolving Communication Difficulties

How then might one deal with difficult listening situations? Whose responsibility is it: the person who has a problem hearing or others? Clearly, there has to be some mutual give and take, but it doesn't always happen that way. What does one do in situations where the listening environment simply is not good? Get up and leave? Try to get people to talk slower? Take steps to avoid getting into such situations in the first place? Why do such situations tend to lead to such embarrassment for all concerned, and why is it almost invariably the responsibility of the deaf or hard of hearing person to make sure that communication flows as smoothly as possible in such situations? Why is this so difficult? It's not that I constantly interact with insensitive or uncaring people. On the contrary, most are exactly the opposite. Yet, it is a constant battle to get people to talk clearly, to turn down the stereo, to take turns while talking, to turn up the lights so it is easier to lipread, to avoid making so much noise that it is difficult to hear, and so on.

The problem is not the people, or even the intentions, but the assumptions people have about what constitutes normal (that is, normative) behavior in various listening situations. When these expectations are not met, the tendency is not to question the validity of the assumptions themselves or the appropriateness of the norms (which people may not even be conscious of) but to blame those who, implicitly or explicitly, do not measure up.

This tendency is certainly not limited to deaf and hard of hearing people. As the downturn in the American economy that began in 2008 clearly showed, one tendency for people who lost their job was to blame themselves for their shortcomings and to find fault with their own performance (and, as myriad newspaper articles attest, to feel embarrassment or shame when seeking assistance, such as emergency food supplies from a food bank). Others, including members of the person's own family, often look at individual characteristics such as motivation and effort to explain why someone is not working or not earning enough to support the family rather than blaming large-scale social and economic changes, such as globalization or a huge reduction in the number of good-paying manufacturing jobs.

I do not suggest that individual characteristics such as motivation, initiative, and drive are unimportant. Indeed, they are crucial to an individual's success. However, if there is one thing that sociologists have shown the world over the past century, it is that such attributes are simply insufficient explanations for success or failure, happiness or sadness, wealth or poverty, or any number of other situations in which people and families might find themselves. There has to be a balance, even if it is not always an equal one, among individual, cultural, and social explanations.*

---

*As an example, one might consider different explanations to the question of why some people are poor. An individual explanation would tend to focus on personal attributes, such as motivation, to explain this condition. A cultural explanation might emphasize that there are certain norms or values (such as a willingness to "defer gratification") that have an impact on whether a person or a family is likely to be poor. A structural or social explanation of poverty would emphasize factors such as the reduced number of good-paying manufacturing jobs in the United States in recent years or the inequitable funding of public schools within and among states. Sociologists tend to emphasize social explanations.

How then can one try to resolve some of the communication difficulties implicit in the thousands of contacts that deaf people, hard of hearing people, and hearing people have with one another on a daily basis? Although there are obviously norms to follow, I would suggest again that many of the norms in these situations are ambiguous and that people frequently are not sure how to behave in these encounters. Consequently, the situation can be defined more easily and managed by the person most willing to take the initiative and make constructive suggestions. This is not a foolproof solution, since some situations are more easily redefined than others, but one factor that could make a difference is whether the person has support from someone else in the effort.

Indirect support for this comes from a series of classic social psychological experiments conducted more than fifty years ago by Solomon Asch. In these experiments, a subject was shown one line and then asked to identify which one of three other lines was the same length as the original. When this task was done individually, there were very few errors because the answer was quite obvious. However, when a number of other people in a group all gave the same incorrect answer, there was pressure on the last subject to conform to the group consensus. Not all of the subjects in these experiments went along with the group, but many did. However, when the experiment was changed so that one person in the group gave the correct answer before it was the subject's turn to respond (while everyone else still gave the same incorrect answer), then the pressure to conform was much less, and few errors were made. In other words, when one had an ally, there was more freedom to challenge the norm of conformity that had been implicitly defined in this experimental situation.[11]

Although this suggestion may not be foolproof either, at least it is a start. I suspect that it is likely to be especially effective when one is with friends and acquaintances and it is relatively easy to ensure that the lighting and acoustics are good, that there is no glare from the sunlight, that a table in a restaurant is in a quiet corner, that people take turns while talking, and so on. Perhaps there is even an inverse relationship here: The less rigid or formal the norms are in a particular setting, the more willing people are to modify their actions to make it easier for people to communicate with one another.

In Summary

It might be useful to summarize some of my comments and observations related to deaf and hard of hearing people, as well as my own experiences, that have appeared in this chapter: Among other things, sociology emphasizes the importance of situations and how situations are defined to help explain why people behave the way they do. This is not to say that other factors, such as our personality or our religious beliefs, are not important. But situational norms, or rules for behavior, are one of the things that sociologists emphasize.

While situations are important determinants of our behavior, it is also true that norms are typically somewhat fragile and arbitrary, and they are often ambiguous as well. Things don't have to be the way they are and, in many cases, ten or twenty or more years ago they weren't.

As we understand more about the arbitrary nature of the norms governing our behavior in various situations it becomes easier to suggest and make changes. Even entrenched norms, such as those reflected in Jim Crow laws in the post–Civil War South (laws that mandated the strict separation of blacks and whites in many aspects of life), can be changed over time, and new laws are frequently an effective way to do this.

Making changes, even if we acknowledge the arbitrary nature of the norms, is still not easy, especially if one has to initiate the changes personally. For one thing, we have to deal with a lifetime of powerful socialization experiences, experiences that may sometimes not equip us to want to take the initiative.

Since it is sometimes difficult to go it alone, it is useful to remember that allies are important. Even if there is a good deal of social pressure to keep quiet and not rock the boat, if just one other person lends support this can quickly change the dynamics of the situation.

In the final analysis, change isn't easy to make, either for a person trying to initiate changes or in terms of actually modifying the norms. Other people may be comfortable with the way things are, powerful people may have a vested interest in maintaining the status quo, people may be unaware of the negative consequences of their actions and resentful if this is pointed out to them, people may be less willing to make changes if they are time-consuming, and so on. Like other lists, this one is virtually endless. However, change does happen, and there is much we can do to encourage those changes that improve various aspects of the lives of deaf and hard of hearing people.

As John Dewey said in *Reconstruction in Philosophy,* "Since changes are going on anyway, the great thing is to learn enough about them so that we will be able to lay hold of them and turn them in the direction of our desires."[12]

Notes

1. David Wright, *Deafness* (New York: Stein and Day, 1969); Henry Kisor, *What's That Pig Outdoors?* (New York: Hill and Wang, 1990). The title of Kisor's book comes from a lipreading misunderstanding. His son asked him, "What's that big loud noise?" That question, and the question posed in the title of his book, appear exactly the same to a lipreader who cannot hear the words.

2. David G. Myers, *A Quiet World: Living with Hearing Loss* (New Haven, Conn.: Yale University Press, 2000).

3. Gina A. Oliva, *Alone in the Mainstream: A Deaf Woman Remembers Public School* (Washington, D.C.: Gallaudet University Press, 2004); Lou Ann Walker, *A Loss for Words: The Story of Deafness in a Family* (New York: Harper Perennial, 1987); R. H. Miller, *Deaf Hearing Boy: A Memoir* (Washington, D.C.: Gallaudet University Press, 2004); Paul Preston, *Mother Father Deaf: Living between Sound and Silence* (Cambridge, Mass.: Harvard University Press, 1994).

4. Michael Chorost, *Rebuilt: My Journey Back to the Hearing World* (Boston: Houghton Mifflin Mariner, 2006); Arlene Romoff, *Hear Again: Back to Life with a Cochlear Implant* (New York: League for the Hard of Hearing, 1999); Beverly Biderman, *Wired for Sound: A Journey into Hearing* (Toronto: Trifolium Books, 1998).

5. Josh Swiller, *The Unheard: A Memoir of Deafness and Africa* (New York: Henry Holt, 2007).

6. Genetic etiologies account for at least 50 percent of congenital hearing loss in children, according to the American Speech-Language-Hearing Association (www.asha.org/public/hearing/disorders/causes.htm). One of the most comprehensive accounts of genetics and deafness is *Genetics, Disability, and Deafness* (Washington, D.C.: Gallaudet University Press, 2002).

7. One of the most important investigations that focuses on this matter is Robert A. Scott's classic study, *The Making of Blind Men: A Study of Adult Socialization* (New York: Russell Sage Foundation, 1969). Scott observes that blindness is a social role that people who cannot see learn how to play, primarily as a consequence of their interaction with various agencies that purport to serve blind people. Implicit in this socialization experience is a conflict between how blind men may see themselves and how "blindness workers" typically perceive them.

8. Stanley Milgram, *Obedience to Authority: An Experimental View* (New York: Harper & Row, 1974).

9. Philip Zimbardo, "Comment: The Pathology of Imprisonment," *Society*, April 1972, p. 4.

10. Myers, *A Quiet World*, p. 99.

11. Solomon E. Asch, "Opinions and Social Pressure," *Scientific American* 193 (1955): 31–35.

12. John Dewey, *Reconstruction in Philosophy*, enlarged ed. (Boston: Beacon Press, 1971), p. 116.

Part II.

My Experiences as a Cochlear Implant User

Cochlear Implants

IN THE LATE 1990s, I began paying more attention to the growing popularity of cochlear implants. I was looking for something interesting to write about, and since cochlear implantation was (and still is) a controversial topic in the Deaf community, I thought that others might be curious about how this relatively new technology worked and who was using and benefiting from it. Initially, my interest in implants centered on the parents of children who were using the device. Why were parents getting cochlear implants for their young children? How did parents become aware of cochlear implants? What did they expect the implant to do for their children? How has it changed their lives and the life of their children? How has the device made a difference in terms of educational and communication choices for their children?

Cochlear implants are designed to help people hear, especially those who get little or no benefit from hearing aids. Implants have been around in one form or another since the first modern attempt to

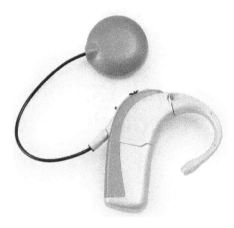

The Advanced Bionics Harmony behind-the-ear cochlear implant.
This is the external portion of the implant. Copyright 2010 Advanced
Bionics Corporation. Reprinted with permission.

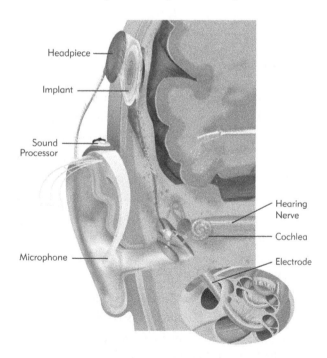

Cross section of the ear showing the internal and some of the external parts
of the cochlear implant. Copyright 2010 Advanced Bionics Corporation.
Reprinted with permission.

electrically stimulate the auditory (hearing) nerve took place in France in the late 1950s. A few adults and children underwent experimental cochlear implant surgery during the next quarter-century, but not until 1984 did the U.S. Food and Drug Administration (FDA) approve an implant for use in deaf adults. Six years later, the FDA approved cochlear implants for use in deaf children from two to seventeen years of age. In 2000, the FDA approved cochlear implantation in the United States for children as young as twelve months.[1] In fact, many children younger than twelve months old (in the United States and abroad) are now receiving implants. Moreover, many deaf children, as well as many adults, are now getting two implants.

A cochlear implant consists of two basic components: Internal parts, which are surgically implanted, and external parts, which together usually look like a behind-the-ear (BTE) hearing aid. The external parts of the implant include a battery, one or two small microphones, a microcomputer, a quarter-sized headpiece that magnetically attaches to an internal receiver, and a short wire that connects the headpiece to the microcomputer as shown in the first illustration on the previous page. The internal components consist of the receiver ("implant" in the second illustration), and a several-inch-long wirelike electrode array that runs from the receiver to the cochlea. Sounds picked up by the microphones are converted into digital information by the microcomputer and instantaneously transmitted via radio waves to the internal receiver and then along the electrode array. The end of the array is inserted into the tiny, pea-sized, fluid-filled cochlea. Ideally, at the end of this process, the auditory nerve fibers in the cochlea are stimulated by the electrical current, and the auditory (hearing) nerve, which runs from the cochlea to the cortex of the brain, is able to transmit sounds to the brain.

Cochlear Implant Research

Gallaudet University's research institute (Gallaudet Research Institute, GRI) has an in-house grant program to support research that reflects priorities set by the university. Among the priorities in the late 1990s were such things as recruitment and retention as well as technologies that could benefit deaf and hard of hearing people. My research interests fit reasonably well into these categories, and I was able to secure the funds necessary to get started.

Successful research is primarily the result of a lot of hard work, but it can also be the result of some good luck, and I was particularly lucky in several important ways. First, at the time I applied for the funding, Lisa Holden-Pitt, a researcher at GRI, was preparing a lengthy questionnaire dealing with many of these same issues. This questionnaire, "Survey of Parents of Pediatric Implantees," was distributed to more than 1,800 families of children with cochlear implants around the country early in 1999. Second, I began a very rewarding and productive professional collaboration with Irene Leigh, a professor and clinical psychologist at Gallaudet, who was also interested in many of these issues.* There were only a few hundred children with an implant in 1990, but by the end of the decade thousands of children had received the device and it was apparent that implantation was here to stay.

Irene and I had some input into the questionnaire, but most of the work had already been done before we began our research. However, we made one important addition: respondents were asked if they would be willing to be contacted about participating in a follow-up interview regarding some of the topics covered in the questionnaire. Dozens of parents who returned the questionnaire indicated they would be willing to talk with us. We subsequently contacted many of them (and a few other parents whose names we got from other sources) and spent the summer and fall of 1999 talking with more than eighty parents in

---

*Irene was identified as deaf on her second birthday and grew up primarily in Chicago, where she developed spoken language by working with a speech and language therapist and by attending public schools that emphasized an oral (nonsigning) tradition. Like me, she was fully mainstreamed in high school, and (unlike me) she had the experience of a homeroom that consisted of deaf students only. Neither of us used sign language as we were growing up. Irene began formally signing in her early twenties (I began when I was thirty).

interviews that lasted, on average, about ninety minutes. Analyses of the interviews and responses to the GRI questionnaire, as well as other issues such as implant technology, ethics, and the changing views of the Deaf community concerning cochlear implants, are discussed in *Cochlear Implants in Children: Ethics and Choices,* published in 2002 and then again in 2005, after we added a brief afterword. Our Gallaudet University colleagues Patricia Spencer, a professor of social work, and Jay Lucker, a professor of audiology, also contributed to the book.

Our research for *Cochlear Implants in Children* took us to fifteen states and one foreign country. Here, too, we were lucky. For one thing, my son Andy, at the time a student at the College of William and Mary, was one of the top 800-meter runners in the nation. He had finished second in the NCAA Division I outdoor track and field national championships in 1997 and was running in that meet again, as a senior, in 1999. The 1999 meet was held at Boise State University in Boise, Idaho, and during breaks in the competition I interviewed several families in that area for the book. Later in the summer, Andy ran in the USA track and field championships in Eugene, Oregon, and again I took the opportunity to interview several more families in Oregon and Washington.

During that summer, I also attended the biennial meetings of the Cochlear Implant Club International (later called Cochlear Implant Association, Inc.) in Los Angeles and arranged to interview a number of families in Southern California. Irene called on family connections in Florida and in the New York City area and interviewed several families there. She also interviewed one family in Australia when she attended the 1999 World Congress of the World Federation of the Deaf in Brisbane. Without these opportunities for broadening our sample, our modest research budget would have limited our study to families within a few hundred miles of Washington, D.C. In these respects, our research certainly came at a propitious time.

Almost all of the interviews Irene and I conducted for the book were held in the homes of the families we talked with. During the course of the interviews, most of the parents realized that I had good speech and could hear most of what they were saying. At the time, I was using two fairly new hearing aids. These aids were not digital aids, but they were programmable, and they enabled me to hear more than I could with older models, especially because I was using two hearing aids for the first time in my life. The interviews were somewhat informal, although we had a long list of questions and covered pretty much the same ground in all of them. Often, either during the interview or at the end, parents asked me if I had ever considered getting an implant for myself. I could honestly say that I had not.

In the fall, I had a sabbatical leave from my teaching responsibilities at Gallaudet and was able to continue our research by interviewing some additional families in other parts of the country. The more I talked with parents and children, as well as with some young adults at Gallaudet who had once used or were still using an implant, the more I began to think about getting one for myself, but I was still a long way from making a decision.

In May 1999, shortly before we got started with our interviews, Irene, Lisa Holden-Pitt, and I visited the Listening Center at Johns Hopkins University in Baltimore, one of the leading cochlear implant centers on the East Coast. Dr. John Niparko, a cochlear implant surgeon and the director of the center, had worked with Lisa and others in the development of the GRI questionnaire, and we wanted a better feel for what actually happened at a cochlear implant center. We had lunch with him and a large group of other surgeons and audiologists and asked them questions about their program and facilities. Although it was interesting to learn more about what goes on in a well-run cochlear implant center, especially the rigorous process of evaluating potential implant recipients, I was not considering an implant for myself at the time.

During the course of the lunch, Sigrid Cerf came into the room where we were meeting, sat unobtrusively near the table, and later talked with us about her experiences as an implant user. Her story appeared in an article in *People* magazine in fall 2000. She was one of the first adults I met who was using and clearly benefitting from the device.*

━━━

Another important event in my evolving personal and professional interest in cochlear implants actually came a few months before our trip to Baltimore, when I moderated a panel discussion about implants at Gallaudet. About a year before this discussion, Dr. I. King Jordan, Gallaudet's president at the time, selected me and Sharon Barnartt, a colleague in the sociology department, as distinguished faculty members in recognition of our book about the 1988 Deaf President Now (DPN) protest.[2] This is an honor that the president of the university bestows on one or two faculty members each year, and we were delighted to receive the award.

One of the requirements for receiving the award was to prepare a lecture or other type of public presentation during the academic year following the award. Since I was interested in cochlear implants, I set up a diverse panel of those who had a cochlear implant and were still using it and those who had implant surgery but were no longer using the device. Sometimes those who have a cochlear implant stop using it because they are not satisfied with the performance. Perhaps they don't like the new sounds, or perhaps they have difficulty perceiving sounds, including voices, while using their implant. Others might decide to stop using their implant because of social pressure from their nonimplanted peers or because they are happy with their identity as a culturally Deaf person and do not see the need for an implant. Since the mid-1980s, there has been significant opposition to cochlear implantation from

---

*Sigrid's husband, Vinton Cerf, one of the real "fathers" of the Internet, is hard of hearing. Among his other accomplishments, he served a term as a member of the Gallaudet University Board of Trustees.

many people with a strong social and cultural connection to the Deaf community. Although this opposition has focused primarily on pediatric implants since the turn of the century, there was still a good deal of general opposition to cochlear implants within the Deaf community at the time I set up the panel in February 1999.

The one nonuser on the panel was Rory Osbrink, a thoughtful and articulate student who had taken a course from me during the fall 1998 semester. In addition to Rory, I asked one of the members of Gallaudet's Board of Trustees, Bill Graham, to participate. Bill, at the time an editor for *World Book Encyclopedia*, had lost his hearing as an adult and had recently received an implant. In addition to these two panelists, I invited two other implant users who had long-standing ties to the Deaf community and were fluent signers. Phil Aiello was one of the first committed members of the Deaf community to explore and ultimately decide to get an implant for himself. He was curious about what sound was like and did not receive much benefit from hearing aids. Myrna (Mo) Aiello, Phil's wife, was initially very opposed to Phil's decision but ultimately went along with it and later even decided to get an implant for herself. The Aiellos were criticized by some in the Deaf community for their decision, but by the time the panel was set up in early 1999, they were very pleased with their decision and remain so today.

I had asked Irene and a few other people on campus who were knowledgeable about cochlear implants to come to the panel discussion. I made a short presentation, which included a brief summary of how a cochlear implant works, before the panel began, and I wanted to be sure that Irene and the others had an opportunity to make any comments related to that, or, if they were so inclined, to respond to any questions from the audience. Irene and I hadn't really started our research yet (that came a few months later), but we were a bit anxious and nervous before the panel got under way, given the negative tempo of the times at Gallaudet related to implants. We didn't stay apprehensive for long, however, as there was an overflow audience, people respectfully listened to or watched the panelists, and there were many questions that would have continued long past the allotted time if that had been an option. As Irene has suggested, perhaps at some level this positive reaction to the panel discussion, as well as to the individual panelists, reassured me that I might not be tarred and feathered if I ever decided to get a cochlear implant for myself.

Also in spring 1999, I attended a cochlear implant conference in South Carolina, where I had a chance to meet some parents of children with implants as well as some researchers and teachers. Here again, although I was not yet thinking about getting one for myself, I learned more about the device and the postsurgery habilitation or rehabilitation that must occur, particularly for children.

Being Evaluated for an Implant

In late fall 1999, I transitioned from thinking about cochlear implants intellectually to thinking about them more personally. I was still busy with the research for the book, but I also actively began exploring the possibility of getting one for myself. In retrospect, it is difficult to identify one single, overriding reason for taking the next step. For one thing, it was clear from my interviews with parents as well as from the research literature that many people were benefiting from the device. Although I was not always certain what the children I met were actually hearing, I met some adults, especially the Aiellos but others as well, who were delighted with the device and encouraged me, if only by example, to investigate it for myself. In addition, people, including professionals in the field, continued to tell me that I would be a good candidate for an implant. I suppose that if one hears the same message often enough, it's not difficult to start believing it.

On a different level, I began to think that there was little to lose and potentially much to gain. For example, until I was about thirty, I was generally able to use a typical voice telephone. Over the next ten years, however, it became increasingly difficult for me to follow a phone conversation, and I needed to use an amplifier on the handset. After the mid-1980s, I pretty much gave up on the phone and either used a TTY* or a relay service, asked someone else to make a call for me, or wrote letters and e-mails. I thought that even if the implant wasn't wonderful, I would still be able to use a TTY, send letters or e-mails, and communicate with my family and friends at about the same level of success. I also was getting tired of enjoying a relatively barrier-free communication environment at work but facing increasingly larger communication problems outside of Gallaudet. Communication with hearing people has always been difficult for me, particularly in group situations and in noisy environments. As it became even more of a chore to communicate with nonsigning friends, acquaintances, and the general public, I began thinking that a cochlear implant might make my life outside of Gallaudet less stressful and more enjoyable.

This communication stress extended to family interaction as well, especially around the dinner table or when my children invited friends over to the house. I never really felt I was as much a part of their lives as I might have been if it had been easier for everyone to communicate (which is partly because I didn't sign at home as much as I should have). I thought that an implant might improve this situation. If it didn't, I would still be able to use a hearing aid in one ear, which is what I had been doing most of my life until I started using two aids in 1998. Consequently, in fall 1999, I began the process of being evaluated for an

---

*A TTY (or TDD, as it is sometimes called) makes it possible for deaf and hard of hearing persons to communicate on the telephone. By using a small, specially designed modem with a small keyboard, users are able to communicate with anyone with a similar device. The abbreviation TTY derives from old teletype machines that were used until smaller devices were developed in the 1970s. Although TTYs were used extensively in the past, new devices and services such as video phones, relay services, e-mail, text messages, video chats, and hand-held pagers have largely taken over the field. Part of the reason I became more dependent on a TTY in the mid-1980s was because my hearing loss became noticeably more pronounced. Perhaps part of the reason for that is because I was careless and spent a day with a jackhammer tearing up some concrete steps in my backyard without wearing proper ear protection: not a good idea.

implant. This process is somewhat tedious, and I had to work not only through a cochlear implant center but also through Kaiser Permanente, my health maintenance organization, which I hoped would pay for the expensive procedure.

—*mm*—

One of the benefits of working at Gallaudet University is that there is an outstanding audiology clinic on campus available for faculty, staff, and students to use free of charge. Moreover, members of the Gallaudet community frequently are able to purchase hearing aids at a considerable savings compared to the price charged by most conventional hearing aid dealers. Over the years, I had many hearing tests and evaluations from the audiologists there, especially Lisa Devlin, and talked with them about various types of hearing aids, including new digital devices, assistive listening devices, and cochlear implants. Consequently, it was easy to see the progression of my sensorineural hearing loss. It certainly wasn't likely that I would be using less powerful aids in the future.

Armed with this evidence, I contacted my personal physician at Kaiser and inquired about being evaluated for a cochlear implant. I had heard from someone that if Kaiser decided to support an implant, the surgery would have to be done at a hospital in Washington, D.C. I wanted clarification about this from the beginning, because I knew that if I went ahead, I wanted the procedure done at Johns Hopkins in Baltimore. After all, we could always change health plans, if necessary, even if this delayed everything for a while. As it turned out, Kaiser did send all their implant patients to Hopkins. They started with me by having one of their in-house audiologists evaluate my hearing. No one was surprised that the results of this evaluation suggested that I would be a potential candidate for an implant.

After my evaluation at Kaiser, I contacted the Listening Center at Hopkins via e-mail, my preferred mode of long-distance communication, about being evaluated there for an implant. I got no response for several months but was in no hurry, so I didn't pursue the matter further at the time. Later, early in 2000, I had some contact with Dr. Niparko, the director of the center, and as part of an e-mail message asked him if anyone had gotten my earlier e-mail and if it might be possible for me to be evaluated for an implant. Soon after, I was contacted by someone from Hopkins about setting up an appointment.

There are a number of steps in the evaluation process at a cochlear implant center. It begins with an initial hearing test similar to the ones I had had at Gallaudet and elsewhere, as well as the one I had a few months before at Kaiser Permanente. In addition, the audiologist who was assigned to me, Jennifer Yeagle, showed me the various implant options. There were basically three devices that were available at the time: Clarion, manufactured by Advanced Bionics Corporation in California; Nucleus 24, manufactured by Cochlear Corporation in Australia; and the Combi 40+, manufactured by Med-El in Austria. Only the first two had been formally approved by the FDA, but I could have selected the Med-El model as part of a clinical trial in which Johns Hopkins was participating. At the time, I was still not ready to make a decision about implantation in general, much less decide which device I wanted.

—*᷄᷄*—

One of the issues that critics of cochlear implants frequently bring up is the presumed pressure from the professional staff at implant centers to get the device. This pressure allegedly occurs because the center needs patients to stay in business, implant companies need to sell the device for the same reason, and because deafness is seen as a "terrible tragedy" that needs to be ameliorated if possible. There was certainly no pressure from my audiologist, the surgeon, or anyone else at Hopkins to get the device. They said that I would be a good or excellent candidate for an implant, but I never got the sense that they felt I would be throwing away a chance at a "normal life" if I decided not to go ahead with the procedure.

This was also an issue that came up in many of the interviews Irene and I had with parents of children with cochlear implants. Parents repeatedly said that they felt little if any pressure from the implant center to get the device. Many parents did say that the audiologists, surgeons, and other health professionals they talked with told them that an implant was likely to be more effective than hearing aids for their deaf child. However, the parents we talked with also consistently said that they had to make the decision by themselves, a decision that was frequently reached after talking with extended family members, other parents of deaf children, and, occasionally, deaf adults and others who were part of the Deaf community. In the final analysis, if they decided against the procedure, that was fine with the center. Some parents even wondered why the implant center wasn't pushing the device more aggressively if it was such a great thing. This was the same basic message I got from the people at Hopkins.

Hair and Air

As I mentioned, there were three implant companies when I started the evaluation process, and this is still true today, more than a decade later. I had had some contact with one of the companies, Advanced Bionics, in summer 1999 when I was in Los Angeles at the Cochlear Implant Club International conference, but I didn't know much about the other two companies. As is the case at many conferences, field trips to organizations, agencies, schools, and the like were available for conference participants. One place I visited was the House Ear Institute, one of the major cochlear implant centers on the West Coast, and I learned more about implants in their well-stocked library and by talking with some of the researchers who worked there. Another place that I could have visited, but was unable to do so because of a time conflict, was Advanced Bionics, located about an hour from downtown Los Angeles. Fortunately, I had met Joanne Syrga, an implant user and insurance reimbursement specialist on the staff of Advanced Bionics, before my trip to Los Angeles. Dr. Lisa Holden-Pitt, my colleague from Gallaudet who was also attending the conference, and I were able to arrange for a special tour a day or two after other conference participants had visited the facilities.

I had never seen how an implant was actually made, and Lisa and I were able to tour the production facilities and meet some of the staff. One of the people I met was Doug Lynch, the marketing director. Doug is also an implant user, and I talked with him about his experiences with the device. Virtually all of the experiences of the implant users, parents, and researchers that I met in Southern California were quite positive, and perhaps this helped nudge me in the direction of more actively investigating the possibility of acquiring an implant for myself.

∼

In summer 2000, about a year after talking with Doug and his colleagues at Advanced Bionics, Jennifer Yeagle showed me another working model of the Advanced Bionics Clarion cochlear implant in her office at Johns Hopkins, as well as samples of the implants made by two other manufacturers, Cochlear Corporation and Med-El. One of the norms among professionals at the Listening Center is to be totally objective about the relative merits of the different devices. Indeed, the phrase "they're all good" was said so many times that I lost count. Never did I hear anyone at Hopkins say that one device was better than another or favor one implant company over another. The decision was mine and mine alone. However, they did give me literature distributed by the three companies and directed me to their Web sites.

Because implant technology continues to evolve at a rapid rate, sometimes people think that it might be better to wait a few months, or longer, until the next generation of implants comes on the market. This is not unlike what happens in other areas where sophisticated electronic equipment is rapidly changing. Indeed, in one of my initial consultations with Dr. Niparko I wondered if it might be a good idea to wait for a while and see what was coming down the pike. He replied that this was certainly an option, but that there had been some recent developments in implant technology and there probably wouldn't be any major new breakthroughs for a while. Thus, at least from that standpoint, this might be as good a time as any to get the device.

After talking with Jennifer in summer 2000 and learning more about the available implant models, and after completing the audiological assessment at Hopkins, I had to decide whether to continue the evaluation process. There were several additional steps, including a physical examination and a CT scan of my inner ear, which needed to be done before I could become an official candidate for an implant. The staff at the Listening Center would then decide whether they felt I was a reasonable prospect, and I would have to decide whether to go under the knife.

One of these additional assessments was a psychological evaluation. This evaluation consisted of some paper-and-pencil psychological tests and an interview with a psychologist on the staff at Hopkins. I drove to Baltimore for this evaluation late in summer 2000. This assessment is designed to evaluate such issues as whether the candidate has a realistic picture of what an implant is likely to do, whether the decision is really the candidate's or whether he or she is doing it to please others, whether a miracle is expected, and so on. Presumably, if the expectations are not realistic, or if the decision is not really one's own, then additional consultations and discussions would be necessary. In my case, because I was not expecting a miracle (and was not encouraged to expect one by anyone at Hopkins) and because I was presumably competent enough to decide on my own whether to go ahead with the surgery, I was not the beneficiary of additional counseling.

Another appointment I had at Hopkins about this time was a follow-up visit with Dr. Niparko to talk about questions I had related to the surgery. I first met him in May 1999 when Lisa, Irene, and I went to the Listening Center to have lunch with the staff and talk about our research. I had also briefly talked with him about surgical issues earlier in the summer after one of my appointments with Jennifer. That appointment was somewhat truncated, however, and I had some additional issues to discuss with him. Also, I wanted Arlene to meet him and get a better understanding of what an implant might do for me. Among the items discussed in the literature I had been given were the possible risks of implant surgery. Some facial nerves are quite close to the cochlea, and there have been some reports of facial paralysis and other damage done by the surgery (temporary facial paralysis—for about two months—had happened to one of the children whose parents I interviewed in summer 1999). I wanted more information and assurance about what was in store for me if I decided to go ahead. During the course of our meeting, it was clear that I was missing some of what Dr. Niparko said. We were discussing hair cells, and I had difficulty distinguishing between the words *hair* and *air*. Although this was hardly surprising, it nevertheless led to a discussion with Arlene about the limitations of hearing with an aid and what it might mean to have an implant. Perhaps, we surmised, with an implant I would be able distinguish between *hair* and *air*. (As it happens, this is still something I'm working on.)

One Sunday afternoon in October 2000, shortly after we met with Dr. Niparko, Arlene and I attended a support group meeting at Johns Hopkins. These meetings occur occasionally and attract cochlear implant users, parents of children with implants, prospective implantees, professional staff, and others. This particular presentation was related to cochlear implants and music and was made by one of the surgical residents who had studied music before deciding to switch to medicine. I still had not decided whether to go ahead with the surgery, but this was yet another opportunity to talk with some implant users and see how they were able to function with the device. It was also an opportunity to listen to some music that was played during the presentation, and I recall telling Arlene that I could hear the sound of music quite clearly with my hearing aids. Consequently, I wondered again what improvements might be in store for me if I decided to go ahead with the implant. In a nutshell, this was a major concern. I was not doing that badly with hearing aids, and I certainly didn't want to make things worse, in terms of hearing voices as well as music and other sounds, if I decided to get an implant. Arlene and I were also able to spend a little time talking about these matters with Dr. Niparko after the presentation. In the end, I left the meeting with the vague feeling that, yes, the aids were reasonably good, especially using two of them, but the implant perhaps would be even better.

—*mm*—

Another of my concerns in fall 2000 was the timing of the surgery. I still had not fully committed to the implant, but if I decided to go ahead the best time would be during a period when I was not teaching classes. The Christmas break extending into mid-January, spring vacation in mid-March, or summer vacation all seemed like good times. The surgery would almost certainly be on an outpatient basis, but because some hair would be shaved off the side of my head and because I would need a few days to recover from the surgery itself, I wanted to be sure an appropriate time would be available. My biggest concern about the timing, however, was that I wasn't too eager to make it obvious to my students at Gallaudet that I had just had implant surgery. Although I had not specifically discussed cochlear implants with my students in my fall classes, I thought that many of them, like many others on campus, might not be inclined to see cochlear implants in a favorable light. Consequently, I didn't want my surgery, the recovery, and the implant itself to detract from the comfortable classroom environment I was trying to create any more than necessary. I mentioned some of my concerns about the timing to Dr. Niparko during our discussion after the presentation at the support group meeting in October, and he said that it would be possible to do it during the Christmas break.

Finally, after spending several more weeks talking with Arlene, our kids, and others, including many of my colleagues and friends at Gallaudet, reading what others were writing about their experiences, and endlessly weighing the pros and cons of getting an implant, I told Jennifer in November that I would go ahead. I also asked them to schedule the surgery during Christmas break, if that was still a possibility; I was soon informed that the date of surgery was December 20, 2000. I also decided to get the Advanced Bionics implant after talking with people that were using it, getting information from the implant companies, and corresponding with Doug Lynch and others about the latest developments in their technology.

About a month before the scheduled surgery, our daughter Amanda was hospitalized with a serious illness for about a week and had to drop out of college. This became the major medical issue for us during the fall, and we decided to postpone the surgery until her medical problem was taken care of.

One of the consequences of postponing the surgery was that I would have to make yet another visit to Hopkins several months later to be re-evaluated. The audiological assessments are only good for six months, so I had to be recertified as audiologically eligible once again. Fortunately, I would not have to go through the psychological assessment again, since my psychological health was presumed to be stable enough to proceed.

Following the holiday season, I again needed to decide whether to go ahead with the surgery, postpone it, or forget about it. In January, Irene and I talked briefly about some of our research findings at a meeting of educators and other professionals at the Laurent Clerc National Deaf Education Center on the Gallaudet campus, which had recently established a new cochlear implant program. We were making good progress on our book while I was going through my own personal decision-making process, and we had this opportunity to informally talk about our research shortly before the spring semester began.

I talked to one former Gallaudet faculty member, Allen Sussman, at this meeting and told him that one of the reasons I was thinking about getting an implant was because I wanted to try to make my non-Gallaudet life less complicated and less stressful. Dr. Sussman, who is a Deaf psychologist, thought that was a pretty good reason for getting an implant; he also had nothing negative to say about my impending decision. In fact, he had participated on a committee, along with Phil and Mo Aiello, Dr. Niparko, and others, charged by the National Association of the Deaf—the premier advocacy organization for Deaf people in the United States—to revise its position paper on cochlear implants.

The original paper, written in the early 1990s, adamantly opposed pediatric cochlear implants. This original paper, implicitly or explicitly, was most likely an important reason why many people in the Deaf community were opposed to cochlear implants in general during the 1990s. Even though the position paper focused on pediatric implants, it was published in an official association newsletter (*NAD Broadcaster*, March 1991), and it is likely that its appearance reinforced some of the negative feelings many Deaf people had about implants for adults. In any case, by the beginning of the new century, many people felt it was time for a new position paper with a more even-handed approach. This new paper was completed in October 2000 and is still posted on the association's Web site (nad.org). The views of the National Association of the Deaf have become more inclusive over the years, and cochlear implants are now seen as one option that parents might reasonably consider for their child.

The conversation with Allen Sussman, as well as additional talks with other implant users, colleagues in the sociology department at Gallaudet, particularly Dick Meisegeier (the same guy who had called me way back in 1977 and offered me the job at Gallaudet), and others finally convinced me that few if any people in the Deaf community or at Gallaudet would see me as a traitor for going ahead with the surgery. If some did, I was confident that I would be able to defend my decision without too much trouble.

Several weeks after the beginning of the new year, I contacted Jennifer again and arranged for another audiological assessment and consultation prior to the surgery. Not surprisingly, in the assessment I again demonstrated that my audiological abilities (especially on word- and sentence-recognition tests) were somewhere between poor and poorer, even with two hearing aids, and I remained qualified for the implant.

In the consultation following my assessment, Jennifer asked me if I was interested in participating in a clinical trial for a new implant model developed by Advanced Bionics. This new device, called the CII Bionic Ear, had to go through a formal testing period mandated by the FDA before it could be made available to the general public. This particular model had programming and electronic capabilities (a "high resolution" speech-processing strategy) that previous models did not have, and many experts in the field thought that this program would eventually prove to be an important advance over existing processing strategies. If I was interested in participating in the trial, it would mean some additional testing, a trip or two to California where the implant was made, and, we hoped, better hearing in the end. It didn't take too much persuading to convince me to participate, especially after I did some Internet research, read all the information included with the informed consent form, and contacted a few professionals involved in its development, nor did it hurt that the company is located near Los Angeles, a nice place to visit.

Ironically, if I had gotten my implant in December, as originally scheduled, I would not have had a chance to participate in the clinical trial. Even though the original surgery date was postponed because of Amanda's illness, in the end it did have a silver lining. Amanda is just fine, too.

Surgery

My cochlear implant surgery was rescheduled for March 2001. Because I wanted to have the surgery at a time when I was not teaching and since I was pretty sure I would be able to be back in the classroom the following week, I decided to go ahead during Gallaudet's spring break.

Before the implant surgery, I had not had surgery for more than thirty years. Although I had confidence in the surgical team at Hopkins and knew it likely would be uneventful, I was still apprehensive. The apprehension was not only medically related; given the nature of my work at Gallaudet, as well as my long-term association with many Deaf people, I still had some social and cultural apprehension as well.

Monday, March 12, 2001, was the last day that I had any residual hearing in my right ear. One important concern of the parents I interviewed was that if their child's implant didn't work, there would be no possibility of going back to a hearing aid in that ear. I was thinking about this as I relaxed in our new Jacuzzi, occasionally putting my head under the water and wondering what it would sound like in a few days when I could try the whirlpool again. I also hoped that a relaxing water massage would make it easier for me to sleep, especially because we were supposed to be at the hospital in Baltimore, about a forty-five-minute drive from our home, by six o'clock the following morning.

I did sleep, although not exactly like a baby, and Arlene and I drove to the Johns Hopkins outpatient center long before the sun came up. After checking in with the surgery receptionist and making it through an hour-long preoperative waiting period, I changed into the unfashionable clothing that I would wear for the surgery. Arlene and I had a little time to talk before I was ushered into the operating room, and Jennifer and a representative from Advanced Bionics also stopped by to say hello and give me moral support. Another visitor was one of the physicians that would be assisting Dr. Niparko. He wanted to know which ear I wanted implanted. I was taken aback by this question because Jennifer and I had agreed several weeks before that my right ear was the best ear for the implant. Selecting the most appropriate ear for a cochlear implant is not an exact science (assuming that the person is only getting one implant), but since there was more residual hearing in my left ear, it made sense to implant the right ear. Also, because I had been using a hearing aid on my right ear for more than thirty years, that ear had a history of "auditory memory" that might be helpful. In any case, I told him the right ear for the implant, although I was tempted to say that I would decide after I got into the operating room.

I also knew that they would need to shave part of my hair off before the surgery. Some of the parents Irene and I had talked with in our research said they were surprised at how much hair their child had lost, but others said just the opposite. The only surprising thing to me at this point was that they didn't do the shaving before putting me to sleep. In addition, they even let me keep my hearing aids on until I was out cold so I could communicate with the attending nurse, who removed her protective mask so I would have no trouble lipreading her instructions.

When I woke up, I was back in the same chair I had been sitting in before being ushered into the operating room. I was told that the surgery had taken about ninety minutes. Anyone who has had surgery knows that it takes some time to shake off the effects of the anesthesia, and I was no exception. It is not a pleasant feeling, but there were no complications, and after taking an hour or two to get enough strength back to walk out the door, Arlene and I were able to leave for home by the early afternoon. We were given some pain medication and antibiotics, and were told to contact them if I experienced any unexpected problems. We also had a small white sticker, about one by three inches, labeled CII BIONIC EAR with the serial number of my newly implanted device. Dr. Niparko had given this to Arlene after the surgery, suggesting that we might want to use it as a bumper sticker. Because it is much too small for the car (and I doubt if anyone who took the time to bend down and read it would understand what it was about anyway), I never figured out what to do with it.

After the surgery, someone in the operating room had taped a large, convex-shaped foam bandage, similar in size to a large headphone, over the area around my right ear, which I needed to keep on for a couple of days. There was no pain, then or later, but it was certainly a little awkward trying to wear my glasses over the large pad. I couldn't hear anything in that ear yet, of course, although I could still use a hearing aid in my left ear. One of our friends, Loretta Saks, brought dinner over that night, and I felt up to eating a full meal. I wasn't quite ready to head for the gym or ride the new bicycle that I had optimistically purchased the day before the surgery, but I felt pretty good and was confident that I would have no trouble teaching again the following week.

Having a new piece of electronic equipment implanted in my head was not something I thought about too much, in spite of my earlier ambivalence about getting an implant. I became more conscious about having a small computer near my ear after reading Michael Chorost's book, *Rebuilt: My Journey Back to the Hearing World* several years later, but at the time I didn't think about it a lot. I simply hoped that when the implant was activated a few weeks after the surgery, I would be able to hear voices and other sounds better than I could with the various hearing aids that I had used for more than thirty-five years.

～～～

The first few days after the surgery were spent at home where, among other things, I had to get used to some new sleeping positions. Normally I liked to sleep on my stomach or my right side, but this obviously wasn't practical or even possible immediately after the surgery. Over the years, I've had some periodic back problems, so trying some new sleep positions wasn't entirely new to me. It took longer to fall asleep on my back, but that's eventually the position that proved to be most comfortable. If one lies there long enough, sleep will eventually come, or at least it did for me.

Arlene and I had to wash the incision and apply some liquid anti-biotics after I took off the bandage two or three days later. This was the first time we were able to see how much hair I was actually missing. It wasn't too bad, especially since I had let my hair grow a bit longer be-fore the surgery. With some creative combing, I was able to cover some of the area that had been shaved. I also discovered that the incision, perhaps reflecting my feelings leading up to the surgery, seemed to be in the shape of a four- or five-inch-long question mark. It was nice (for me and even more for others) that after removing the bandage I was finally able to take a shower. I could even get the incision and the area around the incision wet, although it was a bit swollen and numb. The numbness lasted to some degree for several months. It was also easy to feel the internal receiver that had been implanted under my skin, about an inch from the top of my ear lobe.*

"Hey, You Got a Cochlear Implant!"

A week after the surgery, I was feeling fine and was ready to head back to the classroom. I thought about wearing a baseball cap to try to cover the small shaved spot, but since I had not been in the habit of teaching with a hat on before the surgery, I thought that my students and colleagues might find this a bit odd. Certainly, it would call attention to my head. I eventually decided to put one or two adhesive bandages over the incision and comb some hair over them. This wasn't entirely successful, but it felt like a decent compromise between wearing a hat and doing nothing at all. After a few days, I put on two smaller bandages because the larger ones didn't stick very well. After a few days, I stopped using any covering at all.

Part of the reason for considering the hat and opting for the bandages was that I wasn't eager to make it obvious to my students that I had had cochlear implant surgery. I wasn't sure how they would react, and I didn't want to argue with anyone about my decision yet.

On the first day back after spring vacation, after stopping in the men's room to double-check my appearance, I headed off to class. My first class was a relatively small one entitled Race and Ethnic Relations, which consisted primarily of upper-division students. I walked into the room, not knowing what to expect, and the first thing a student said

---

*The length of the incision and the amount of hair that is removed is not a constant in cochlear implant surgery, although since my surgery in 2001 the incisions have generally gotten smaller.

(signed) to me was, "Hey, you got a cochlear implant!" At least he didn't add, "you traitor!" Obviously I had to say something, so I just said that he was right and that I hoped it would enable me to hear better than I could with hearing aids. Several other students were in the room by then, and we talked about it a little. To my relief, there was no animosity at all, no one walked out, and we soon started talking about whatever the topic was for the day. That proved to be the attitude expressed by almost everyone at Gallaudet after the surgery: curiosity, even indifference, but no hostility, and in some cases interest in exploring the possibility of implant surgery for themselves. (In fact, a number of my former colleagues at Gallaudet as well as members of their families have gotten cochlear implants during the past several years.)

The next day I taught Introduction to Sociology, a course made up primarily of lower-division students, and I thought that perhaps there would be some negative comments from them. This time no one, including me, said anything at all about the implant. Later in the semester, after I had my implant activated and it was clear from the wires and body-worn speech processor that I was using a cochlear implant, we discussed the issue a bit. But here, too, there was no criticism from the students (even after I turned in the final grades). Perhaps some of the students didn't say anything critical because they were apprehensive that because I was responsible for evaluating their performance in the course, I would hold it against them. Although this is a possibility, the fact that there were no criticisms at all, in informal discussions or on the anonymous course evaluations at the end of the semester, leads me to conclude that it was not a major issue for them.

Several of my colleagues commented on how inconspicuous the loss of hair was. Perhaps I was self-conscious, but their comments made it much easier for me to take off the adhesive bandages and not worry about what it looked like, especially since it was a temporary condition.

I had no postsurgical complications, and the wound healed quickly. The only noticeable aftereffect was the numbness around the incision, and I had to clean the area around the newly implanted device for a few weeks. I was looking forward to having the implant activated in mid-April and finding out how the equipment worked; implants are turned on and programmed (or "mapped") a few weeks after the surgery. The area needs time for the swelling to go down before the external components can be magnetically attached to the internal receiver. I managed to get by using only a hearing aid on my left ear, something that was not very satisfactory. Because I didn't need to hear much at Gallaudet anyway, the month passed fairly quickly. However, I did bang the right (implanted) side of my head on a taxicab door before the implant was activated, but I hoped that this wouldn't have any effect on the implanted receiver, which is protected in a ceramic casing.

Turning It On

One day before my implant was activated, Irene and I again presented our research at the Laurent Clerc National Deaf Education Center on campus. Part of this center, the Kendall Demonstration Elementary School, is for deaf and hard of hearing children of pre–high school age. The school had recently established a cochlear implant center, and Debra Nussbaum, the director of the center, invited us to talk to teachers and staff about our research. This was a straightforward presentation, but I did end by mentioning that I had had cochlear implant surgery a few weeks before and that I would find out the next day if it worked. Some people were obviously surprised and curious, but again, there was no hostility. In fact, some of those I met that day said they were considering implant surgery for themselves, and I invited anyone who wanted to know how it all turned out to send me an e-mail.

The activation process is somewhat tedious, and, at least at Johns Hopkins, includes a two-hour session one day followed by an equally long session a day or two later. Another session is about two weeks after that. Arlene joined me the first day because she was very curious to see what would happen. Jennifer began by having me attach the external microphone to the internal receiver. This was not too difficult to do since it is magnetically connected, but the strength of the magnet has to be adjusted so that it isn't too loose or too tight. This was easily accomplished in a matter of minutes. Then Jennifer began the process of introducing some sounds to the device and making sure that all the electrodes worked.

Among other things, I was asked to identify how loud or soft various pure tones were. The mapping or programming process entails letting the audiologist know when the tone is first heard, and how it progresses from soft to something approaching a comfortable loudness level. This takes some time because it has to be done for each electrode pair in the array; in my case, it had to be done eight times. Then, there was something Jennifer called a "sweep," when all the tones were played back at the levels I deemed them to be comfortable and further adjustments were made.

The parents Irene and I had talked with in our research said that their child's audiologist started by gradually introducing very quiet sounds so that the newly implanted child would not be overwhelmed by the experience. Adult implantees I had talked with said the same thing, so I was not surprised that it took a while for me to hear some sounds through the implant. Nor was I particularly surprised that the kinds of things I could hear were a far cry from what I defined as "normal hearing." Of course, for me, normal hearing was what I could hear with my hearing aids, and what I was able to hear with the implant the first day was not what I would call normal by any stretch of the imagination. In fact, the buzzes and beeps and other weird sounds that I heard were, to say the least, disappointing. Intellectually, I knew that it was unlikely that on the first day I would clearly understand voices and pick up sounds that I had not heard before. Emotionally, I naturally wanted to be a "superstar" and to be able to hear and understand conversations right away. Needless to say, this didn't happen. After going through the slow process of identifying pure tones, I was eventually able to hear Jennifer clap and bang her hand on the table, but her voice, and the voices of others, had a squeaky quality with little depth or resonance. In fact, after the two hours were up, I was beginning to wonder what I had gotten myself into and if this was going to work out as I had hoped. On a more positive note, it was clear, even on the first day, that I was responding to sounds in the high-frequency range that I had not been able to hear when I was using a hearing aid.

During the session, Dr. Niparko's nurse came into Jennifer's office to check on my incision to be sure that everything was healing normally. On that score, everything was fine. Jennifer also said that Dr. Niparko himself might come in and see how things were going. I interpreted this to mean that if I did well then he would come. Because he didn't come and there was no explanation about why he didn't, I thought that perhaps it was because there wasn't much for me to show him. There was probably another explanation, but I left feeling that this was going to take a lot longer than I had hoped.

—*um*—

On the drive home with Arlene after the initial activation, we had the radio on and I could hear very little. I could not make out any of the conversation, either on the radio or with her. I remember banging on the car door, perhaps out of frustration, and even that I could barely hear. I had gone from wearing two relatively unobtrusive hearing aids that, although far from perfect, at least made it possible to know the car radio was on and to hear when I banged the car door, to wearing a strange device attached to my belt (a body-worn microcomputer/speech processor) with a cord running under my shirt to a microphone that was magnetically attached to another electronic device implanted in my head. I was beginning to wonder how much more progress like this I could stand. I'm sometimes not the most patient person in the world, but I'm pretty realistic and more or less objective, and I was having a hard time seeing how this was going to get much better for quite a while. I wasn't ready to make any optimistic predictions, especially, as someone once said, about the future.

After we got home, I had to go to Gallaudet for an evening class. For the second day in a row, Irene and I had been asked to talk about our research, this time to a graduate class in social work taught by Patricia Spencer, who has done a lot of research on pediatric cochlear implants and contributed an excellent chapter to the book Irene and I were still working on. Pat was not able to attend this particular class, but she had told the students that I had gotten an implant, that it would be activated a few hours before I arrived, and that I would be able to tell them what the first day was like. Irene had already started talking about our research before I showed up (I told her I would be late), and she and the others in the class were anxious to find out what happened that day at Hopkins. I tried to be as upbeat as possible, but I'm also sure that my initial disappointment came through in my comments. Irene has reminded me several times since then that I was complaining about how Arlene's voice sounded; in fact, Irene said I told her that I couldn't tell the difference between her voice and Arlene's voice. Irene is profoundly deaf, but she often uses her voice, and the distinction between her voice and Arlene's is one that I could easily make when I was using the hearing aids I had before the surgery. The students in the class had a number of questions for me about the surgery and the activation process, but I don't recall many of them (even though they were in ASL and most of the students were not using their voice anyway), probably because I was somewhat down in the dumps and wanted to move on to a discussion of our research.

The next day I drove by myself back to Hopkins for the second mapping session. Sometimes word- and sentence-recognition tests are given in a soundproof room before a new mapping session, but for this second session that didn't happen. Instead, adjustments were made after my responses, or lack thereof, to pure tones, words, and conversation in Jennifer's office. Although I was able to tolerate more sound during the second mapping session than I was the day before, I was certainly not able to carry on a conversation without lipreading.

—*mm*—

There are several speech-processing strategies or programs that one can use with a cochlear implant. Each implant manufacturer has some unique programs, and some are fairly common to all. In my case, I needed to choose between three general programs.* Because there was enough memory space on the body-worn speech processor I was using for all three programs, each of them was adjusted for my needs and then loaded into the processor. I periodically changed programs and tried to decide which one I liked best. After experimenting for a while, one of the programs sounded more like what I defined as "natural" than the other two, and I stayed with that one until new software was activated a few months later.

One of the keys to success with the implant is to practice listening to familiar and unfamiliar sounds and voices as often as possible and to wear the implant whenever possible. When I was wearing hearing aids, I usually wanted to take them off for several hours each day, and I often did things around the house without using the aids. This was primarily because ear molds can be irritating, and it is difficult to leave them in the ear canal for hours each day, day after day, especially during the hot and humid summer months. This practice did not make it any easier for us to communicate around the house, and it often led to a lot of walking and running up and down the stairs when it was necessary to get someone's attention. At least it helped keep us all in shape! With an implant, there is nothing in the ear canal, and it is consequently much easier to leave it on all day. The batteries have to be changed from time

---

*Processing strategies essentially involve making decisions about how the electrodes on the array inserted into the cochlea are activated to stimulate the auditory nerve fibers located there. New strategies are being developed all the time, and more recent implant models typically use different programs than the ones available in 2001. (Chapter 2 in Christiansen and Leigh, *Cochlear Implants in Children: Ethics and Choices*, written by Jay R. Lucker, includes a more detailed discussion about cochlear implant technology and processing strategies.)

to time, but since they usually last for many hours, this doesn't need to be done very often.

—*m*—

At the time my implant was activated in April 2001, the only Advanced Bionics model that was available was a body-worn speech processor. On this model, which a few people still use today, the processor is about the size of a deck of cards and is placed in a small leather or canvas pouch with a metal clip that can be attached to the user's belt. A thin insulated cord connects the processor to the microphone, which is then magnetically attached to the internal receiver. This cord could be left outside one's shirt or blouse, but the most practical thing to do is to weave it under the shirt and string it, along with the microphone, up to the receiver. This takes some getting used to, and unless the cord is attached to one's collar by a small clip, the microphone can easily come off when the user moves around too much. Moreover, a long cord protruding from one's head looks a bit odd. I realized later that one could wear an undershirt and affix the clip to the undershirt, which resulted in a less visible and less obtrusive cord. I quickly came to understand why some parents I interviewed in 1999, whose children were using the Advanced Bionics body-worn processor, were enthusiastic about getting a behind-the-ear model for their child when it became available. The children and adolescents were looking forward to this, too. This was especially true for the young women; it is difficult to wear a dress and a body-worn speech processor at the same time. Moreover, for everyone with a body-worn processor, using the toilet requires new skills not normally covered in the toilet-training chapter of the toddler socialization process. Traveling, too, was somewhat of a nuisance, and like many implant users I was delighted to try out the behind-the-ear model that became available from Advanced Bionics about six months after my surgery.

During my early experiments with the body-worn speech processor, I discovered that I seemed to hear better when I was using a small, auxiliary, lapel microphone. This microphone plugged into the processor, and then I clipped it to the front of my shirt near my neck. This was yet another wire, and I was not particularly comfortable with or excited about two wires snaking up my chest. It was possible to program the speech processor so that all of the sound came through the lapel mic, but I found that an even split between the lapel microphone and the one magnetically attached to the side of my head seemed to work best. On one hand, even if it was cumbersome and time-consuming to put on all this equipment, this arrangement gave me more confidence to approach others and try to communicate with them (especially because the lapel microphone picked up more sound directly in front of me and helped me monitor my own voice more effectively). On the other hand, the microphones, wires, and body-worn processor made it obvious to other people that I was a person with a disability. Although I had been wearing a hearing aid for so long that I didn't think too much about this, I can understand why some users of the body-worn processor might be self-conscious about the visible hardware attached to one's head and clothing. In this respect, the behind-the-ear model has some obvious advantages over the body-worn model.

In fall 2001, when I was still using my body-processor, I attended a volleyball tournament in Pennsylvania with Arlene and Amanda, who was playing for her college team, St. Mary's College of Maryland. During a break in the action, I walked outside and had a nice conversation with someone who was waiting for a football game to start in a few hours. As I later said to Arlene, I wouldn't have had the courage to initiate that type of conversation before I had the implant. Moreover, because I was using the lapel microphone, it made the conversation more natural since I didn't have to ask this person to repeat anything. The communication environment helped as well—a quiet, sunny, early autumn Saturday morning with few cars on the street and no noisy fans in the stands.

Later that day, I asked a bartender about the score of a football game on television, and it was easy to understand what he told me.

— *um* —

For the past several years, the Listening Center at Johns Hopkins has hosted a picnic for implantees, prospective implantees, their families, staff members, and others. I attended the first picnic in 2000, before getting my implant, and talked with some people who already had one about their experiences. I was still in my fact-finding mode at the time, and I said to someone as I was leaving: "I feel like I'm taking a good college course, leaving more confused than when I arrived." The next picnic was in June 2001, about two months after my implant was activated, and I talked to one of the audiologists who worked for Advanced Bionics, the company that made my implant, and told her that my program was "almost there" but still needed more adjustments. I felt that all it would take were some small changes here and there and things would be great.

Here and there, unfortunately, lasted much longer than I initially thought it would. Although I'm sure that the program I have now is much better than the one I was using in 2001, I still sometimes feel that it is not quite there yet, and I continue to need minor adjustments every year or so. I'm realizing that for me, success as an implant user seems to be defined in terms of the incremental progress of the journey rather than some difficult-to-identify final destination. That is, each time I visit Hopkins, changes are made that are small yet noticeable improvements, but after getting used to the new program, it always seems that there is still a little left to be done. Perhaps the only way to see much of a change at this point would be to get another implant on my left ear.

One of the endearing characteristics of all the audiologists and other health professionals at Hopkins, as well as many of my fellow implant users, especially Phil and Mo Aiello, is their upbeat, positive attitude.

Jennifer, for example, has always assured me that I'm doing fine, that everyone is different, that the brain has to get used to the new sounds, and so on. This is all well and good, but it isn't very scientific, and during my first few years with the device, I had a difficult time squaring my experiences with the experiences that seemingly more successful implant users were having with their cochlear implants.

During late summer 2001, I was getting a bit impatient with my progress, especially on the sentence-recognition tests, and I thought it might be a good idea to start some listening therapy. There were listening therapists on the staff of the Listening Center in Baltimore and at a center in suburban Washington, D.C. There was a waiting list at the suburban location, but I could see a therapist right away in Baltimore. Because there was not a lot of difference in terms of time and distance and because the therapy would be relatively short-term, I decided to see someone at the Listening Center. I had to wait until I received permission from Kaiser Permanente, but that proved easy to get, and I began eight weeks of listening therapy with Kristen Ceh in August. This therapy consisted of practicing my new listening skills, since my speech was already quite good. Among other things, I was encouraged to do simple things on the phone, such as ordering pizza or other take-out food. If there was a miscommunication and the person on the other end hung up, so what? Although this therapy was helpful, talking on the phone is still something I do only reluctantly, usually when I initiate the call or know who is calling. (Caller ID is great in this regard.) I also occasionally use voice carryover relay services—more on that later. In addition, I find it easier to use a cell phone than a regular landline telephone. However, the easiest thing of all is to rely on e-mail or text messaging. This is somewhat frustrating, as I expected to be a better phone user after the implant than I've turned out to be.

Journey through Europe

In July, Arlene and I, along with our daughter Amanda, flew to Europe for a three-week vacation. Our sons Erik and Andy were already in Europe, and we decided to take advantage of a unique opportunity for all five of us to spend some time together in Italy. This trip would also give me another opportunity to see how I was doing with my implant.

Arlene, Amanda, and I spent several enjoyable days sightseeing in Paris before taking a train to Switzerland. We spent several days in Montreaux, located a few miles east of Lausanne on the shores of Lake Geneva, and were able to attend a performance by Bobby McFerrin and Chick Corea at the Montreaux Jazz Festival. I was hoping that the implant would make it possible for me to enjoy the performance more than I would have if I was still using my hearing aids. Perhaps it would be easier to listen to jazz than to some other types of music, such as a more complex full-orchestra concert, which I wasn't able to appreciate very much at this point with the implant.

It was not a very satisfying evening in Montreaux in several respects. First, we had to stand up almost the whole time, more than two hours. Also, the music did not sound very pleasant. I'm sure that part of the reason for this is because the acoustics in the cavernous hall were not the best, but I was disappointed that I couldn't appreciate the performance more. I initially thought that if I were using hearing aids instead of an implant I would have at least heard the music more clearly. I was almost certainly wrong, however, because the amplification from the aids would probably have made everything much too loud. When I thought about some of the musical performances I had attended before getting my implant, I realized that it was difficult to hear and appreciate the music unless the audience was fairly quiet and the acoustics in the room were good. Because this was not the case at Montreaux, I suspect that my inability to enjoy all that jazz had more to do with the nature of the room than with the performance of the implant. A sensitivity dial on my body-worn processor did make it possible to reduce some of the background noise, but overall I hoped for more clarity three months after the implant was activated.

Following our short visit to Switzerland, which included a cog-train ride up a nearby mountain with a gorgeous view of Lake Geneva, the three of us got on the train for Rome, where we met Erik and Andy near Castel Sant' Angelo (St. Angelo's Castle—well known to those who have read the book or seen the movie *Demons and Angels*), not too far from Vatican City. I had been to Rome once before, in summer 1967 on my way back from the Philippines, and visited this castle then. Although I don't remember saying to myself in the midsixties that this would be a great place to bring my family, it did turn out to be a convenient place to find each other. We had made reservations at a nearby hotel, but since our arrival times were spread out over several hours, we wanted to make good use of our time and start seeing the sights. It was also good in another respect as well: there were several outdoor amateur musical performances near the castle, and this gave me yet another chance to find out what I could hear with the implant. Perhaps, I thought, music in Italy would sound better than music in Switzerland.

Unfortunately, the music wasn't any more enjoyable for me in Rome than it had been in Montreaux. Because I couldn't blame the acoustics in the hall this time, I realized that it would take a while for me to find a type of music that was pleasant to listen to. Later that evening, we walked over to St. Peter's Square in Vatican City. There was no midnight music there (it was quiet and almost deserted), and it was relatively easy to have a nice conversation with my family in another location I had visited more than thirty years before. It wasn't perfect by any means, however, as their voices still sounded somewhat artificial and had a distinct nasal quality to them.

――――

We left Rome in a rental car and drove north to Tuscany, where we spent a few days in an old monastery that had been converted into a

Erik, Andy, John, Arlene, and Amanda in December 2009.

hotel. From there we traveled to Pisa, Florence, and some of the historic hill towns in that remarkably beautiful part of the world. Although I was able to have conversations with my family during this period (except in the car, where it was not easy to hear, drive, and figure out the confusing road signs at the same time), I didn't attempt to talk too much with others and still didn't notice any dramatic improvement from what I recalled hearing while using hearing aids. Things were getting better, but the progress was slow, unpredictable, and often exasperating. It was obvious to me that it would take longer than I expected to adjust to and benefit from the implant.

In addition to seeing the usual sites in central Italy, we also had an unfortunate car accident while driving from our hotel in Tuscany to Pisa on the Mediterranean coast. We were driving south of Livorno, which is also on the coast about twenty miles from of Pisa, and were hit by another car. The accident was serious enough to involve the local police, and we spent several hours dealing with the accident itself and subsequently getting another rental car. Because we did not speak

Italian and almost no one, including the man who hit our car or the police, spoke much English, this was a bit of a challenge. However, it was not as frustrating as it could have been. In fact, at times it was almost enjoyable. First, the view from a restaurant near the accident site on a cliff overlooking the Mediterranean on the western shore of Italy was breathtaking. It was late afternoon, the restaurant was not crowded, and the sun's oblique rays reflected off the calm, brilliantly blue water several hundred feet below us. Second, and contrary to any stereotypes we might have had about Italians, everyone was calm, helpful, and friendly, including the other driver and his wife, who arrived at the restaurant shortly after the accident. Nothing was rushed, the bar was open, and we leisurely filled out forms and then more forms. No one was hurt, the police called the car rental agency and asked them to stay open past their usual closing time so that we could get another car, hugs were exchanged all around, and the cops even escorted us to the agency (at least five miles away) so we wouldn't get lost. We were able to get another car, drive to the Leaning Tower of Pisa before dark, have an enjoyable dinner in that beautiful city, and drive back to Tuscany.

Unfortunately, as my kids have reminded me, driving back to Tuscany quite late in the evening with a tired and frustrated father who was still trying to adjust to his cochlear implant was no picnic for them or for Arlene. I was driving, it was difficult for anyone to read the map in the dark, the road signs were even more difficult to see and interpret at night than they were during the day, I made a wrong turn off the autostrada (because I didn't get good directions from the novice navigators, of course), and so on. However, with characteristic good humor, they finally got me to pull over so we could figure out where we were and find our way back to the hotel. Fortunately, global positioning technology has contributed to marital and family harmony by making it easier for us to avoid these headaches today; it also helps that my latest cochlear implant hardware and software make it much easier for me to communicate with passengers in the car in 2010 than it was in 2001.

So, what does this *incidente d'auto* have to do with my cochlear implant? Except for the stressful drive back to the hotel, probably not much, since few people involved in the accident and its aftermath spoke much English and no one in our family could speak Italian. Because we all had difficulty understanding each other, we were all on equal footing. However, again it was difficult for me to see how the implant had made much of a difference in my hearing compared to my preimplant days. It would have been difficult to communicate with those who spoke accented English while I was wearing hearing aids, and so it was when I was using the implant. In the back of my mind I had hoped that with an implant I wouldn't have to leave conversations like this to Arlene. If that was one of the goals, I was far from achieving that in Italy (or in France or Switzerland) in summer 2001.

High Resolution

Soon after we returned from Europe, Arlene and I flew to Los Angeles to meet with several audiologists and other professionals at Advanced Bionics. I was participating in the FDA clinical trial for a new speech-processing program, and we went to California to have this software activated. It was also an opportunity to get personal attention that few implant users enjoy.

I worked with a few audiologists and software engineers at Advanced Bionics, who spent a couple of days trying variations of this new program. One of the problems that implantees sometimes experience is temporary facial twitching when the volume is turned up too high. Some of the facial nerves are located close to the cochlea, and when the current is too strong or the array is too close to the facial nerves this can cause some problems. This was an ongoing issue for me, and it was particularly noticeable in California. In fact, in one situation, after making some adjustments in the programming, the twitching in my right eye became so pronounced that I grabbed the external receiver and yanked it off my head. The audiologists seemed fascinated.

After the audiologists at Advanced Bionics made adjustments to the program and put me through some rather tedious listening tests, Arlene and I went out to lunch or dinner or both to see how it all worked in "real life." At the time I was still using the body-worn processor, and because three different programs can be stored on the device I was able to go back and forth among the different variations to see which ones seemed to work best. Some of them were not very good, at least for me, and at a restaurant one evening with Arlene and our son Andy, who was just starting law school at UCLA, I felt particularly tired and depressed and could make out very little of what they were saying. Part of the problem is that the mapping is done in a very quiet room, and the real world is, to say the least, somewhat different. After several days of this, I left with some variations of the new high resolution program that seemed to be promising, and we returned to Maryland. However, I was still disappointed; it was difficult to understand people even in fairly quiet rooms, and using the telephone comfortably still appeared to be a long way off.

On the way back from Los Angeles, we stopped in Minneapolis for my niece's wedding. Arlene and I arrived late in the evening the day before the wedding, but not in time to attend the rehearsal dinner. We did run into my brother Dave and some of his family in the hotel lobby before going to our room, and we were able to talk with some of the other guests, including my sister-in-law Sally's parents, whom I had not seen for many years. As it happens, Sally's father had developed a significant hearing loss and was very interested in my cochlear implant.

Later in the evening, Arlene and I went to the bar in the hotel and ran into other people I had known years before in Wisconsin but hadn't seen since the Nixon administration. As always, it was very difficult for me to communicate with them in the noisy, dark bar, but Arlene interpreted much of the conversation, and we shared some of what we had been up to over the years.

The wedding was the next day, and in the various challenging communication situations that occurred throughout the day there was again no discernible difference between my pre- and post-implant communication success. It was frustrating to try to talk with people at the church after the wedding, or at the dinner, because the background noise made it all but impossible to understand the conversations. Of course, background noise was a persistent problem when I was using hearing aids. The sensitivity dial on my speech processor reduced some of this annoying problem but didn't eliminate it, and it proved to be very difficult to understand individual voices with all the other random noises coming in as well. The only time I could clearly hear someone was when the person spoke, usually unintentionally, directly into the microphone on the side of my head.

The question that invariably comes up in difficult listening situations for hard of hearing people is this: How does one deal with these ambiguous situations? I mentioned before that this happened more frequently than I would like to remember while I was growing up in Salt Lake City, in college and graduate school, and in various pre-Gallaudet academic settings. One strategy for dealing with this is to pretend that one is hearing something when one is not, but bluffing, as noted earlier, is not a good idea. Another strategy is to ask the person to repeat the comment or question until it is understood. This has its limitations. I've learned that in general most people are not particularly interested in taking the time to repeat what they've said, especially more than once. Moreover, if there are a number of other people around that a hearing person could converse with more comfortably, it is not surprising that many hearing people will eventually seek out those folks. Writing back and forth is a possibility, but this is time-consuming and is not likely to lead to a long or rich and satisfying conversation. Perhaps the most frustrating thing for me, as well as for many deaf and hard of hearing people, is that I sincerely want to communicate with other people, but the logistics, the acoustics, and the norms of the situation frequently make it difficult to do so. When I've raised this issue in conversations with others, often their first reaction is sure, we would be glad to take the time to talk, we'll move to a quiet place, and so on. But, after the novelty wears off, this is seldom done consistently. One of the reasons I decided to try a cochlear implant was to make my conversations with nonsigning hearing people more satisfying and less stressful. Although this was still my goal, by the end of the first summer with the device it was still an elusive one.

Family Matters

In fall 2001, I got a behind-the-ear model to replace the body-worn external processor that I had been using since my cochlear implant was activated in April. This model is much easier to put on in the morning than the body-worn processor, since all one needs to do is place the headpiece on the internal receiver and affix the rest of the device over the ear. It looks very much like a conventional hearing aid. One problem with the original Advanced Bionics model was that the toggle-switch control was awkward to use, and at the beginning it was difficult to switch programs and adjust the volume level. I used the original behind-the-ear model that I got in 2001 until mid-2009 (although it was replaced once or twice, thankfully under the warranty). On the newer behind-the-ear model, called the Harmony, these adjustments are easier to make. (The Harmony model is shown in the illustration at the beginning of this chapter.)

At first, I did not particularly like the behind-the-ear processor because the sound quality was not equivalent to what I was experiencing with the body-worn processor. I used the new device at a party celebrating the publication of our book at Irene's home in January 2002, and it was more difficult for me to hear and understand what people were saying than it had been a few months earlier while I was using the body-worn model. Eventually, however, convenience won out, and I soon stopped using the body processor altogether. Moreover, the sound quality I perceive with the newer Harmony model I use today is much better than it was with the first behind-the-ear model I started using in late 2001. I still have the old body processor, though, and every time I venture to Hopkins for a program evaluation I take it with me. Jennifer Yeagle, who is still my audiologist there after all these years, reprograms it and, when I get home, I put it back in the closet where it serves as a faithful backup, just in case.

———⁓⁓⁓———

Soon after I received my implant, I started listening to some tapes of books for children to see if that would help me improve my listening skills. Unfortunately, many of these tapes have music as well as voices on them, and this made it difficult to understand some of the words. Some tapes, like the American history series by Jean Fritz, worked pretty well for me. Her books are written for fourth or fifth graders, and the tapes came with the book, so it was possible to follow along. I actually learned something about Patrick Henry, John Hancock, and Plymouth Rock by listening to these tapes. Generally, it was easy for me to follow the words on tape when I had the book in front of me; it was more difficult to understand the words without looking at the book. It would also get somewhat discouraging when long sentences would go by and I would not understand more than a word or two. Although I seldom listen to Jean Fritz or anyone else on tape these days, my ability to understand the words on tape (or on a compact disc) is much better now than it was during my first year with the implant. In fact, after not listening to tapes for several years, I tried again in 2009, listening to a reading of the book *Mike Milligan and Mary Anne*, one of my kids' all-time favorites. I was pleasantly surprised that I could understand virtually every word without even looking at the book.

During the first year with the implant, I got plenty of practice listening to and sometimes trying to repeat words, phrases, and sentences spoken by Arlene and our son Erik, who stayed with us for a few weeks in late 2001 after spending a couple of years teaching English in Japan (and before starting graduate school at the University of Maryland).

Family Matters
by Erik Christiansen

During the period when my dad was listening to a lot of children's books on tape, we also tried "live" readings, where I would sit behind him (so he couldn't read my lips) and read aloud. This method was more flexible than using a tape recorder and was especially advantageous when he missed a few words or started to get lost. It also offered all of the disadvantages that one might expect when two adult males with limited patience and no relevant training were determined to quickly master any and all difficulties introduced by the implant.

One evening in particular stands out. I don't recall the book, but as I read he was having a harder time than usual following along. His requests for me to repeat what I was reading became increasingly strident, and I couldn't prevent myself from becoming resentful that my efforts were being met with such ire. He eventually said something about why it wasn't working, which I took as criticism, and I replied that, hard as it was, he didn't have to be nasty about it. That ended our session.

We made up later than night and had a nice hug, but he never asked me to read to him again. Although it seems obvious, it can take a tremendous amount of patience and understanding, not just from the implantee but also (especially) from family and friends who want to be supportive but don't always know how. A cochlear implant will affect the whole family, and it is necessary for *everyone* to be prepared for that.

Among other things, we practiced a list of words I had gotten from the Listening Center at Hopkins, as well as time-tested spondee words (two syllable words with an equal emphasis or stress on both syllables): baseball, toothpaste, airplane, hot dog, cowboy, outside, railroad, and so on. Sometimes these sessions produced a certain amount of tension, as Erik recounts in the accompanying box.

By the end of 2001, I was a semisatisfied cochlear implant user. In some ways, especially in noisy situations, the implant seemed better than a hearing aid, but in other ways I was disappointed. Piano music, for example, still did not sound very good with the implant (worse than with a hearing aid), although other music, such as jazz, sounded quite pleasant. The acoustical environment made more of a difference for me while using the implant than it did when I was using hearing aids. If the acoustics in the room were quite good, then the implant worked very well. If the acoustics were not good, such as in a room with hardwood floors and bare walls, the performance of the implant deteriorated quite a bit. The very good to not-so-good range for the implant was much wider than a comparable range for a hearing aid, at least at the beginning.

No Superstar

Recently, many people who have received a cochlear implant have written books about their experiences. Most of these books describe fairly positive experiences with the device. People who have gotten an implant and who have not been pleased with it are not likely to spend much time writing about it. However, in the future more deaf and severely hard of hearing adults are likely to contemplate implant surgery (as are parents of deaf children), so any insights and experiences that users, including me, have are likely to give potential implantees some idea about what's in store for them. Clearly, no two people are alike, so any person's implant experience will not be a duplicate of anyone else's. Nevertheless, the more people are aware of the range of experiences that implant users have, the more they can gauge whether they want this for themselves or their child.

In her book *Hear Again*, Arlene Romoff describes, in the form of an almost-daily diary, how she adapted to her cochlear implant during her first year with the device. She writes that at the end of her very first programming session she "could understand random sentences spoken

by the audiologist, without looking." After the first programming session! She could also understand most of what her husband said in the
car without looking at him and most of a weather report on the radio.
Needless to say, it took me a lot longer than one programming session
to reach those milestones; in fact, it took me several years to arrive at
that stage. The sound of voices had a very artificial and nasal quality
for at least the first year, and it took even longer for voices, as well as
many other sounds, to have much of the resonance that I remembered
hearing when I was using hearing aids. For example, soon after I started
using two hearing aids, about eighteen months before I got my implant,
I could hear and feel a deep and satisfying low engine hum or vibration
when I was shifting gears in my car. This low-frequency hum was largely
absent after I started using my implant. (Because of the structure of the
cochlea and the nature of implant surgery, it is frequently easier to hear
high-frequency sounds than low-frequency ones.)

After a year with the device, Romoff writes that she could understand
almost all of the sentences in quiet and moderate noise when she was
tested by her audiologist. She also notes that her pure-tone audiogram
showed that she functioned like a person with a mild hearing loss.

In spite of many success stories such as this, it is still difficult to predict how much any one person, especially an adult, will benefit from
the device. I know adults who have benefited tremendously from the
device; they probably have done about as well as Romoff. I've talked
with others, however, who have not been able to hear very well at all
after getting the implant, even after repeated programming changes. If
someone has a long history as a hearing person, becomes deaf or severely
hard of hearing later in life, and gets an implant without a long delay,
the chances are very good that this person will significantly benefit from
the device. Also, if a hard of hearing person has used a hearing aid for
a long period of time before getting an implant and consequently has
at least had some experience hearing voices and other sounds (that is,
has some auditory memory), then this individual is also likely to do
fairly well with a cochlear implant. On the other hand, if someone has

never heard much sound, has seldom or ever used his or her own voice, and decides as an adult to get an implant, the chances of a Romoff-like experience are about as good as winning the lottery. There are undoubtedly exceptions to these generalizations, however, and predicting success with an implant is still an inexact science.

A few other people who have gotten a cochlear implant have written about their experiences. In his book *Rebuilt,* Michael Chorost describes how the implant dramatically changed his life and enabled him to experience the world in ways that were not available to him before his surgery. A few years after he got his first implant, he decided to get another one so he could enjoy the advantages of bilateral implantation, and he has chronicled his experiences on his Web site. Others have written articles in popular publications such as *Hearing Loss,* a bimonthly magazine published by the Hearing Loss Association of America (formerly SHHH, Self-Help for Hard of Hearing People).

During the first year with the device, it was clear that I would not be a superstar. Even though Jennifer and others at Johns Hopkins assured me that I was doing fine, I continuously compared myself with others who had an implant as well as with those anonymous subjects, reported in the literature, who seemed to be doing better than I was. Because I was used to doing things well and didn't like to come in second, this was a sobering realization. However, I've always thought of myself as the proverbial tortoise rather than the hare, so I resolved to stick with the program and see where things might end up.

Ten Years Later

After a decade with a cochlear implant, has the implant helped me understand hearing and speaking people, especially my wife and children, better? What about noisy situations, especially because those are frequently difficult for hearing aid and implant users? What about hearing tests in a soundproof room? Although these tests are artificial by design, they do provide a comparative measure, so it is easy to see how things change from one year to the next. Most important, would I do it again?

In regards to the hearing tests, one test is designed only to determine the lowest decibel level at which one can hear a sound at different frequencies, whereas other tests are designed to determine if the user can hear and understand words and/or sentences, either in a completely silent environment or with artificial background noise. Like many deaf and hard of hearing people, I've taken many of these tests, but the most revealing difference is a comparison between my last test as a hearing aid user and the various tests I've had while using an implant. As a hearing aid user, I was unable to understand many of the words or sentences; this was true many years ago and was true immediately before my implant surgery. This was one of the most important reasons I decided to go ahead with the surgery: What did I have to lose? If I wasn't hearing many words and sentences in the soundproof room with an aid, having implant surgery, even if it was not very successful, was not going to make things any worse.

Shortly after my implant was activated in 2001, I heard pure tones across all frequencies at the 25–30 dB level. This put me squarely in the mild to moderate hard of hearing range and is a common level of success among new implant users. Over the years, this has remained constant: my pure-tone audiogram taken in 2009 is virtually identical to the one from 2001. The two audiograms shown here represent a "before and after" comparison; the first one was done in 1989 and the second in 2008. According to Jennifer Yeagle, my audiologist at Hopkins, an audiogram is a picture or chart of hearing with decibels (loudness) on the *y* or vertical axis and hertz (Hz, frequency/pitch) on the *x* or horizontal axis. The symbols plotted on the audiogram represent the softest sound heard at each given frequency.

The first audiogram represents unaided hearing; that is, hearing without amplification. I was not using a hearing aid for this hearing test. In

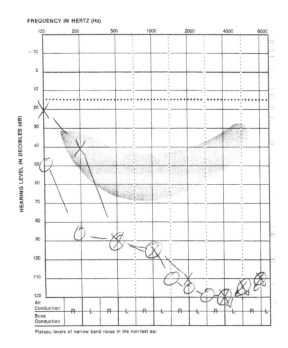

FREQUENCY IN HERTZ (Hz)

A 1989 audiogram of *both* ears *without* a hearing aid.

this steeply sloping audiogram, the X represents the left ear and the O represents the right ear. The difficult-to-see "smile" or "speech banana" in the center of the chart is an approximation of where normal speech sounds occur; I heard a pure tone in the moderate hearing loss range without amplification in my left ear at 250 Hz (a deep bass voice) only at 40 dB (moderately loud). A hearing aid would make it possible to hear the middle frequencies at a lower (quieter) decibel level, putting them in the speech range, but I would still have been unable to hear the higher frequencies, because there was nothing there to amplify.

The second audiogram was done while I was using my implant. In this case, it is clear that I heard higher frequency sounds quite well, as measured by the "S" across the audiogram at about 25–30 dB. (This audiogram did not measure my left ear; a recent audiogram of my left ear shows that my unaided hearing in that ear is about where my right ear was in the late 1980s.)

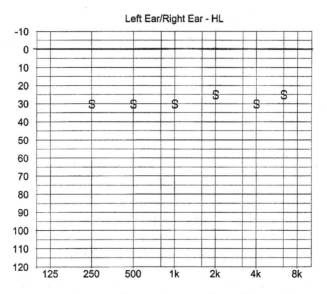

A 2008 audiogram of my *right* ear *with* a cochlear implant.

The situation is more complex for word and sentence discrimination. Hearing pure tones isn't the same thing as hearing and understanding voices, especially in noisy conditions, and cochlear implant users vary tremendously in their ability to hear in such situations. In fall 2002, for example, about eighteen months after I began using my cochlear implant, I identified about 45 percent of the words in the sentences Jennifer read to me in a quiet, soundproof room at Hopkins. Since I knew that some other implant users were doing better, I was disappointed. However, it was many times better than what I was able to do with one or even two hearing aids. After three years with the device, this percentage increased to about 70 percent in quiet situations and approximately 45 percent when artificial noise was introduced. More recent tests show that I recognize about 75 percent of words in quiet situations and a little more than 65 percent when artificial noise is introduced. Thus, although results are not yet perfect, I can hear much better than I could a decade ago, before I had the surgery.

What about the other, real-life situations? The situation is much murkier. On one hand, it is nice to hear things I couldn't hear, or had difficulty hearing, before I got the implant. On the other hand, communicating with other people, especially in situations where several people are talking at once is still no picnic, especially when there is a lot of background noise or if the acoustics of the room are not very good. Things have improved over the years, with new hardware and software (programming) changes, but challenging communication situations have not been eliminated.

One example is Thanksgiving, especially Thanksgiving as we celebrated it for a few years after I got my implant. Dinner was served in a large dining room in a home with poor acoustics and approximately two dozen people, some of whom I didn't know well, in attendance. Many of the people at these dinners, though, were friends and family members, and since they were more aware of my communication problems in such situations, it was easier to talk with them than with relative strangers. However, it was still difficult to participate in anything more than a conversation with whomever happened to be sitting next to me.

My only real solution to communication difficulties in settings like this is to find a quiet corner and talk with someone one on one. Even armed with ideas about what could be done to reduce the level of background noise and make it easier for everyone to communicate more comfortably, it is sometimes difficult to put them into practice. Asking the host to improve the acoustics by putting more curtains on the windows or installing some carpet on the floors is likely to be a nonstarter, even if it's someone I know well. Reminding people not to talk at the same time is difficult to do in large groups and is impossible when young children are present.

The best solution for me is to celebrate Thanksgiving with a smaller group in a smaller dining room with better acoustics. We now do this at home, with curtains over the windows and a large rug on the hardwood floor to improve the listening situation. This makes it much easier to have a conversation with others in my family and makes the entire dinner more enjoyable and satisfying for everyone. There are still the inevitable problems of people not waiting to talk until the previous speaker is done, not talking loudly enough, and talking with their mouth full, but the implant and the improved listening situation has made a difficult communication environment much better.

—*m*—

In the years since I got my cochlear implant, Arlene and I have taken several trips abroad and to Alaska, and these are good opportunities to determine whether the implant has made it easier for me to interact with hearing folks than when I was using hearing aids. I mentioned that during our trip to Europe in summer 2001, shortly after my implant was activated, communication and interaction weren't so great, but in trips since then it has been better. In summer 2004, for example, we took a small-ship cruise to Alaska. This trip was particularly meaningful because my parents lived in Ketchikan many years ago and we were excited about seeing where they had lived and worked. In fact, we found the church where my dad had been the pastor, which is now a National Public Radio station. There was even a small historical marker in the window that described the history of the building, including a brief comment about my father's ministry there in the late 1930s.

One of the side trips included in this cruise was a visit to Glacier Bay National Park. The group flew from Juneau to a small airport near the park, stayed overnight in a lodge, and spent several very chilly hours the next day on a boat observing birds, bears, whales, and glaciers around the bay. We had dinner with a couple from New Zealand while at the lodge, and because of the noise and their accents I had a very difficult time understanding them. Since this was three years after I got the implant, I was frustrated and had to rely on Arlene to interpret much of what they were saying.

Ever since we both started learning to sign in 1977, Arlene has been extremely good about interpreting for me, and does it quite well, but by this time I had hoped not to have to depend on her in situations like this. Many deaf and hard of hearing people face some ambivalence and uncertainty in such situations about how much to reveal, including our communication needs and preferences, to complete strangers or, as was the case in the noisy, dark bar before my niece's Minneapolis wedding, to people we barely know and haven't seen for years. How much do we want to manage the situation ourselves, and how much we want to rely on someone else? These are lifelong conundrums, and I still have difficulty resolving them. I'm fortunate to be married to someone who has taught me a lot of patience and who has never hesitated to help me get through difficult listening situations, even when I'm hesitant to ask for her assistance. Arlene has also put up with my ambivalent feelings about the whole thing, not knowing when I might resent or resist her offer to help. Has this put some stress on our marriage? Yes, but it also has enhanced it because we constantly work to ensure that misunderstandings, and the disagreements and tensions that can arise from them, don't fester and become even bigger problems in the future.

Following our trip to Glacier Bay, the group was bused to the airport for the short flight back to Juneau. We were waiting in the small terminal for the plane to arrive, and, when it did arrive, I was looking out the window and thinking, "Wow, this plane has certainly taxied very close to the building." The plane was a midsize jet and was no more than twenty-five feet from the terminal. However, I assumed that Alaskan pilots must be pretty good, and this guy probably knew what he was doing. After we boarded the flight, the plane started taxing to the runway, and part of one wing broke off as it clipped the terminal! Arlene and I were seated on the other side of the plane, but passengers who could see what had happened immediately got up and started shouting that the pilot needed to stop the plane. Unfortunately, it took several minutes for a flight attendant to call the cockpit and get the pilot to stop. After a while, the plane taxied back to the terminal and we all disembarked. Apparently the airline was not used to having their planes hit terminals, and there was no immediate backup; we had to wait several hours before they figured out what to do.

Finally, after plenty of complaints from the passengers, the airline rounded up a bunch of Alaskan bush pilots and, in small single-engine propeller planes, flew us back to Juneau. This was actually quite nice because it was still light outside (thanks to the long hours of daylight in the summer in the high latitudes) and the plane flew quite low over the water. After we arrived back in Juneau, I met the wife of one of the guys who had flown in the plane with Arlene and me. She was Edith Burns, an audiologist from Boulder, Colorado, and we began a nice friendship with her and her husband that has continued to this day. Since it was very easy to hear and communicate with them, the rest of the cruise was much more enjoyable than the frustrating dinner I had the first night. In fact, several days later as we were walking around Saxman Native Totem Village south of Ketchikan, Edith asked me if I might like to come to Colorado to talk to audiologists and others about the cochlear implant research that Irene Leigh and I were doing. I went to Breckenridge in fall 2005 and again in fall 2006 to talk at two conferences in this breathtakingly beautiful part of the country. Especially at the 2006 conference, I easily heard the questions from the audience and, I hope, responded appropriately. Certainly, audiologists are likely to be among the easiest people to understand since they have a lot of practice speaking clearly and distinctly, but it was nevertheless encouraging to me that I was doing quite well with the implant, at least in an acoustically friendly environment, five years after getting the device.

~~~

In general, in situations with a large group and in a large room, or in a noisy environment (and especially in situations where all three conditions occur), there is still not a huge difference before and after getting the implant in terms of what I can hear and understand. However, in other situations, I see a definite improvement. I mentioned earlier that I've come to enjoy certain types of music since I began using a cochlear implant. In particular, it is much easier to hear and recognize musical instruments such as the flute, the trumpet, and the piccolo. These are instruments (especially the flute) that I did not hear much if at all while using my hearing aid. With the new Harmony BTE device that I've been using since summer 2009 (along with a new processing program), words have even more clarity, and I'm able to have conversations in the car and in fairly quiet rooms as long as people speak reasonably clearly.* I'm also able to hear the car radio quite well, especially the newscasts and programs such as the Diane Rehm show on National Public Radio, where the host speaks very slowly. Other programs, such as "A Prairie Home Companion," and the vocals in virtually all musical selections are still not easy for me to understand.

Finally, what about the last question of whether I would elect to have cochlear implant surgery again? If I had to assign a letter grade to my decade-long experience with an implant, I would give it a B+. Like all final grades, this is a composite of many different tests. While the implant clearly deserves an A on some of the evaluations (especially for high-pitched sounds and communicating with other people one on one in a quiet room), on other evaluations the grade is not so high (using the phone, for example, or conversing in noisy situations). Overall, I've

---

*An additional reason for the increased clarity is because of the placement of the so-called T-Mic microphone on the Harmony BTE device. As can be seen in the second illustration at the beginning of this chapter, the T-Mic is located at the end of the earhook. This places it directly outside the ear canal and makes for a clearer and richer sound than when sounds and voices are picked up solely by a built-in microphone located at the top of the model. (It is also possible to have sounds captured by both microphones.) Perhaps one reason why the sounds seem clearer and richer when using the T-Mic is because this enables the outer ear, or pinna, to serve its intended function: capturing sounds and channeling them towards the ear canal where the T-Mic can easily pick them up and send them to the microcomputer.

been very pleased with my implant and, knowing what I know now, would certainly do it again.

The Vision Thing

For people who are deaf or hard of hearing, the sense of vision inevitably becomes increasingly important for everyday tasks, as well as for access to information and for communicating with others. This is not to suggest that deaf and hard of hearing people naturally develop enhanced visual abilities to compensate for their hearing loss, only that the loss or diminution of one sense means that we rely more on whatever senses remain. Of these, vision reigns paramount, and I, like many of my peers, am primarily a visual learner. For me, seeing is almost a prerequisite to believing.

Even though I have relied on my eyes more than my ears for most of my life, I did not think much about this before January 2006, when I developed a severe case of shingles. Although shingles can appear virtually anywhere (but only on one side of an infected person's body), for me the telltale rash, complete with blisters, pain, and itching, appeared on the left side of my face. The disease was diagnosed early, and I immediately began eye drops, ointment, and other medication, but the vision in my left eye was compromised and I had difficulty seeing things in that eye for more than two years. During that period, I came to appreciate the value of sight, especially for a deaf or hard of hearing person, even more than I had before. I also came to appreciate the value of my cochlear implant and realized that even if I lost my sight, it would be easier to continue to do many of the things I enjoy doing, including listening to music and to the radio, than it would be if I were still using hearing aids. Fortunately, after two surgeries, my left eye is in reasonably good shape (20/25 corrected vision in that eye, compared to not seeing the big E on the Snellen eye chart—or the chart either, for that matter), and I'm doing what I can to make sure I don't get shingles again. If you are a candidate for the shingles vaccine and haven't gotten it yet (if you are sixty or older and had chicken pox as a child), call your doctor tomorrow.

Unlike Diamonds, Warranties Are Not Forever

In spring 2009, I received a letter from Advanced Bionics informing me that the old behind-the-ear model I had been using for more than seven years was becoming obsolete and that the company would not manufacture or repair the device in the very near future. To encourage users to upgrade to a newer external device (the Harmony), the company increased the standard three-year warranty by another two years. One advantage of the Harmony is that it has the capacity to handle a new program called Fidelity 120. This would presumably result in better hearing in general and, more specifically, better understanding of speech in more challenging listening situations. I had tried this new program a year or so before I got the letter, when I was using my body-worn processor in Jennfier Yeagle's office during an annual program adjustment. Although my old behind-the-ear model did not have the capacity to use the new Fidelity 120 program, the reliable old body-worn processor did. Unfortunately, the eye-twitching problem that I experienced while in the clinical trial at Advanced Bionic's headquarters in California returned when I tried using the new enhanced program. Because any type of twitching indicates that the facial nerve is inadvertently stimulated, I was not able to use the new program.

The letter from Advanced Bionics included helpful information about how to get the process started, how much the new device would cost, and other matters. Because I did not want to be stuck with a device that could not be repaired, I decided to contact them. Of course, I didn't want to pay for the new Harmony model myself; rather, I wanted Kaiser Permanente to pay for at least part of the cost of the new equipment. In the end, I was able to get the device, but the process was not smooth and raises some disturbing questions about how cochlear implant users will replace the external equipment when it wears out or becomes obsolete.

First, there was the typical administrative confusion when two bureaucracies are involved: the cochlear implant manufacturer and the health maintenance organization. Referrals were needed, people got sick, e-mails and telephone messages were overlooked or misplaced, and so on: about what I expected. Finally, one of the insurance representatives at Advanced Bionics talked with someone in a position of authority at Kaiser, and Kaiser agreed to pay for the device. Arlene and I were delighted. Unfortunately, a few days later it became apparent that Kaiser was only willing to pay 50 percent of the cost of the new processor. Because the equipment cost $8,000, that meant we would have to come up with a cool $4K. Kaiser considers a cochlear implant to be "durable medical equipment," and, as such, I would have to pay half of their allowance. Although cochlear implants are not specifically listed as an example of such equipment in the benefits brochure (portable commodes, among other things, are), this is how they are classified. This news led to more time-consuming phone calls, faxes, letters, and e-mails to convince Kaiser to pay more of the cost. One obvious argument was that because they paid for the original surgery and equipment, they should also pay for new external processors when the older models become dated or otherwise wear out. It doesn't make medical sense to refuse to pay for a necessary upgrade, or to pay only a portion of the cost, under such conditions. Although the internal components of the implant generally do not need to be replaced, the external components do occasionally need to be changed.

Finally, we tried a different approach to convince Kaiser to pay the entire bill: I had double coverage, and thus Kaiser was both my primary and my secondary insurer. As a faculty member at Gallaudet, I had an individual plan with Kaiser through the Federal Employees Health Benefits (FEHB) program. As a public school teacher in Maryland, Arlene had a family plan with Kaiser available through the Montgomery County Public Schools. Thus, we argued, with the two plans Kaiser should be willing to pay the entire $8,000. In the end, they agreed to do so, and I got the new Harmony processor in June. Surprisingly enough, I am able to use the new Fidelity 120 program with my new device without experiencing any of the eye-twitching problems that bothered me in the past.

I can't help but wonder if Kaiser's decision to pay the full cost of my new device is commonplace among insurance carriers and health maintenance organizations or whether satisfactory resolutions such as this require persistence, wherewithal, and skill to deal with intimidating and sometimes recalcitrant bureaucracies. If the latter, this might not bode well for many of the thousands of implantees who will periodically need to upgrade or replace their external equipment in the years to come. Unlike diamonds, warranties are not forever.

A Close Encounter of the Wrong Kind

I enjoy riding my bicycle; in fact, one could say I'm obsessed with the activity. Like most children, I started riding a bicycle at an early age and even enjoyed taking an occasional long bike ride as a teenager along the foothills of the Wasatch Mountains near our home in Salt Lake. But this was nothing like what I've been doing since the mid-1980s. My first decent bike was a Cannondale aluminum touring bike, and I rode that for many years. Then, in 2001, a day before I had cochlear implant surgery, I bought a Trek recumbent bike (where the rider sits upright on a chair-like seat rather than on a more traditional saddle-like seat). I've had periodic problems with my back over the years, and the manager of my local bike shop assured me that a recumbent bike was much more forgiving for the back than a regular road or touring bike with its signature drop handlebars. I used to enjoy playing tennis but had to give it up when the unpredictable stops and starts began playing havoc with my back. Cycling proved to be a more than adequate substitute. In fact, it was even better than tennis because it could be done alone; I didn't need a partner to get some exercise.

I used the recumbent bike quite a bit from 2001 to 2007, when I got a touring bike made by Rivendell Bicycles. The recumbent was getting a bit tiresome, especially since it was impossible to stand up for leverage when climbing hills. I still use it occasionally but have come to prefer my new bike, which is convenient in another way as well: it is much easier to turn around and see if there is anything behind me on a road bike than on a recumbent bicycle. (This was especially important before I had surgery in my left eye.) I always ride with a small mirror attached to my sunglasses or my helmet, but I usually double check to see that there are no cars or trucks coming behind me by turning around when changing lanes because I can't hear them approaching. I was particularly attracted to the Rivendell bike for two reasons: the braking system, which includes brake levers on two different places on the handlebar for each brake, front and rear, and the fact that the handlebar and the seat could be adjusted to be approximately the same height (usually, on racing or touring bikes the handlebar is much lower than the seat). I thought this would be good for my back and, indeed, it has been.

—*mm*—

Over the past quarter-century I have ridden more than fifty thousand miles, virtually all of which have been without using either a hearing aid or my cochlear implant. Before I got my implant, I had been riding for many years, and for most of that time could hear enough to know if a fire truck or an ambulance was behind me. After getting the implant, however, I was not able to hear sirens or anything else. Some of the experiences while I've been on my bike have been scary, especially recently, and I decided I needed to try using a hearing aid again on my nonimplanted ear.

Because of the location of the internal receiver and the headpiece on my head, it is not practical for me to wear a bicycle helmet and a cochlear implant at the same time. In addition, because the external behind-the-ear cochlear implant can easily become disengaged from the implanted magnet on the internal receiver, it may be more likely to be damaged in the event of a fall than a behind-the-ear hearing aid would be. I was recently involved in an automobile accident when another driver fell asleep and rear-ended my car. The impact was jarring, but I had stopped for a red light and the other driver's speed was not excessive. Even so, my BTE implant literally flew off my head and ended up under the passenger seat of the car (and it took me about five minutes of frantic searching to find it). If I had been using a hearing aid with an earmold instead, I doubt if the aid would have ended up under the seat (or anywhere else).

Two things happened on the (for me) inappropriately named Good Luck Road, a fairly but not excessively busy road not too far from my home. In one case, I was riding when a car pulled up next to me and suddenly someone reached out and punched me in the arm. Fortunately, it wasn't hard enough to knock me off my bike, but it was certainly unexpected and definitely not appreciated. About the same time, and not far from the same location on the same road, I was blissfully riding along and someone in the passenger seat of a car that slowly crept past me pulled out a gun and waved it around. I don't know if this was a starter pistol or the real thing, but he didn't pull the trigger in any event. Because I couldn't hear anything, I have no idea if either of these drivers had been honking to get me to move over, had otherwise tried to get my attention, or were just fooling around.

On some occasions when I've ridden with a friend, there have been situations where drivers have tried to get our attention, either by persistently honking, shouting something (typically unprintable), or gesturing. The only reason I know this is because the other person I've ridden with has been hearing and told me about it. One time in northern Virginia, Vic Van Cleve, a former Gallaudet colleague and longtime friend, and I were riding, and a driver was pounding on the horn and yelling at us to move off the road. I was oblivious to the whole thing, but I can imagine that if Vic hadn't told me to move over the driver would have been even more furious. Has something like this happened when I was out riding alone? It must have.

However, the most dangerous and scary situations did not occur when I was around drivers who felt that bicyclists were, at best, a nuisance. One of the routes I often take on my bike is to ride from my home in University Park, Maryland, to the Beltsville Agricultural Research Center, a multiacre agricultural center operated by the U.S. Department of Agriculture, that is about eight miles (or thirty minutes by bike) away. Although there are some well-traveled roads around the center, many of the other roads have few cars on them, and it is a fairly popular place to ride for cyclists who live in my neck of the woods (which includes thousands of students at the nearby University of Maryland). In fact, I'm pretty sure that somewhere in the research center was where former president George W. Bush often rode his bike. Unfortunately, or fortunately as the case may be, I never ran into him (presumably because he didn't ride on the public roads), even though there must have been times when we were both riding in the same general area.

To get to the roads that run through the research center, I usually ride near the College Park Metrorail stop, about a mile from my home, which is adjacent to two train tracks typically used by freight trains and commuter passenger trains. There is a very primitive stop for the commuter trains where I ride across the tracks. Passengers and others can

Looking north with a train approaching on the right track.

Looking south with the tunnel under the elevated Metrorail stop in the center of the photograph.

walk across the tracks, but there is no crossing signal or station. When approaching the crossing on a bicycle, especially from the south as I usually do, it is fairly easy to see north (to the left in the first photograph, with the train approaching) but not so easy to see south because there are trees and shrubs separating the tracks from the parallel side street (in the second photograph).

Generally, I slow down when approaching the railroad tracks but do not stop, glancing first north to my left and then, as I ride past the trees, south to my right. By the time I turn my head right, I'm usually very close to the first track, which is pretty much too late to stop even if I wanted to. In addition, the trains, especially the freight trains, typically create a lot of vibration, and I assumed I could feel the earth shake when one was approaching, even if I couldn't hear the horn. I have walked near the railroad crossing many times and have always felt I was able to tell, by vibrations alone, when a train was coming. Over the years, I concluded that my early-warning system, such as it was, was adequate and that I would have time to see if there were any trains approaching before riding across the tracks on my bike. Plus, it only took a second to ride across the tracks, so I wasn't too worried about it or even thought much about it.

The first time my dubious methodology was called into question was a couple of years ago when, after I got close to the first track, I could see that a fast-approaching freight train from the south was only about two hundred feet away from me. I assume the engineer must have been using the train's horn to warn me to get out of the way, but I didn't hear anything. Obviously, there was nothing else the engineer could have done; he (or perhaps she) couldn't have slammed on the brakes. Luckily for me, I saw the train in time and quickly peddled past the tracks toward the tunnel under the adjacent Metrorail tracks, visible in the back of the second photograph. The train was on the second of the two parallel tracks. That is, as I was crossing the first track on my bicycle I could see the train rapidly approaching from the south on the second track. Even if it had been right in front of me, I still could have stopped because I was riding very slowly. In any case, although this was somewhat traumatic, I thought it was a one-time occurrence and didn't think too much about it until recently.

There is a tendency in life to become complacent, to follow the path of least resistance as it were, especially when the usual way of doing something seems to be good enough and there doesn't seem to be any particular reason to change. Consequently, for several years after this close encounter with the oncoming locomotive, I continued to approach the crossing in my usual way. Sometimes I could see a train headlight off in the distance, but it was usually a long way off and I assumed that if anything was closer I would be able to feel it.

One weekday morning in September 2009, soon after I retired from Gallaudet, I decided to enjoy my newfound freedom by taking a bicycle ride at a time when I would have been teaching a class or working in my office a few months earlier. I was anticipating riding some variation of my usual route around the agricultural center and approached the railroad crossing in College Park in my usual lackadaisical way. I looked to my left, to see if there was any sign of a train coming from the north and, because there wasn't, started to cross the first track. Then I looked to my right and was terrified to see a train was bearing down on me, unexpectedly on the first track. It was no more than fifty feet or so away and showing no sign of slowing down. (That is, the train was about the same distance from the crossing as the train in the first photo, and on the same track, but going in the opposite direction.) By this time, I was in the center of the track and peddled as hard as I could to get out of the way. (Fortunately, I hadn't disengaged my biking shoes from the pedals; if I had, it would have been very difficult to get off the track.) Since I'm still around to write about it, I obviously made it safely past the oncoming train, but I was pretty shook up by the experience and almost ran into another biker coming the other way through the tunnel.

As was the case a few years earlier, I'm sure the engineer was madly pulling the cord or pushing the button or whatever they do to activate the horn. As before, I was oblivious to the whole thing. I was surprised that I had not felt the vibrations from the train at all and realized that my early-warning system left much to be desired. I was also surprised, and somewhat angry as well, that the engineer was obviously driving the train on the "wrong" track. The trains I've seen on these tracks have always followed the American way of driving on the right. (I've seen a number of trains on these tracks since this incident, and they were all—well, all but one anyway—on the right track.) Why was the engineer driving the train on the left? I quickly concluded that if I wanted to enjoy my retirement years, something would have to change.

The day before this ride, I had my annual cochlear implant evaluation with Jennifer Yeagle at Johns Hopkins. I had been using the new Harmony model for about three months, and it was time to see if it needed some adjustments. We talked about bilateral implantation, which has become more popular among adult implant users during the past few years. (It has also become popular for young children.) Jennifer said that if I ever decided to pursue another implant, I should begin by using a hearing aid in my nonimplanted ear. I had stopped using hearing aids in 2001 after I got my implant, and over the years I gave away my old aids. I particularly did not like having to use an ear mold, which often did not fit very well and caused a lot of annoying whistling, and I was getting such good results from my implant that I never really missed the aids. Many people do use an implant and a hearing aid together, and although I never liked it before, perhaps with the improvements in hearing aid technology it was time to try it again. In any case, that was what I was thinking about when I left Hopkins after our appointment.

After my experience with the oncoming train the next day, I thought it wise to put the new hearing aid plan into fast-forward mode and find something to use while riding my bike. Although it might be nice to have a hearing aid that could also be used while I was wearing my cochlear implant, it was a lot more important to try to find something to use when biking, especially since I have no intention of giving that up. I quickly contacted my personal physician, who gave me a referral to an audiologist. It took a few months, but since January 2010 I have been riding my bike while using a Phonak digital hearing aid on my nonimplanted ear. Although not perfect, it does enable me to hear oncoming trains, fire engines, and many of the other potential hazards that bike riders face each day. In addition, using a hearing aid while riding makes it easier to adhere to an important norm of cycling: offering assistance to another rider who is stranded on the side of the road, often with a flat tire. (It also makes it easier for me to respond to motorists who frequently ask for directions.)

Relay Services

What are some lessons one can gain from this experience, apart from the obvious "stop, look, and (if possible) listen" reminder that many of us relegate to the back burner especially when nothing traumatic happens to cause us to change our behavior? Clearly, the world for deaf and hard of hearing people can be an inconvenient and sometimes precarious place, even if we don't always admit it. Most of the time, the inconveniences are minor and can be managed without too much effort. This is especially true since the passage of the Americans with Disabilities Act in 1990, which has given deaf and hard of hearing people more communication options than existed before. One such option focuses on relay services. When using this option, the deaf or hard of hearing caller calls the service, typically using a TTY, a personal computer (sometimes with a camera so the user can simply sign the message), or another device, and the relay service operator calls the number of the hearing person the deaf caller wishes to talk with. Then, the operator relays the hearing person's comments to the deaf person and serves as a communications link between the two parties.

One variation of this system that I frequently use is called *voice carryover*. In this scenario, I contact the relay service on my personal computer and type the number I want to call. The relay service then initiates the call by first calling my home phone number. I pick up the phone and say hello, and then the relay operator calls the number of the party I want to contact. When the other person picks up the phone, the operator types what the person says, I read this on my computer, and then I respond by talking into the phone. This works only if the deaf or hard of hearing user has a voice that can be understood by someone on the other end of the line. Because people can generally understand me without a problem, this system usually works for me. When using voice carryover, the other party's voice is heard by the relay operator and the caller, to the extent the caller can hear on the phone. Because I can hear much of what the other person says on the phone by holding the phone near the microphone on my cochlear implant, it is a good system for me, and the typed comments by the relay operator frequently serve as backup.

It is not a perfect system by any means, since the words typed by the operator are always several seconds behind what the other person on the phone says. Moreover, people do not always talk clearly on the phone. There are frequently some awkward pauses in the conversation, and I sometimes have to ask the person to repeat the comment so the relay operator can catch up. In addition, when I'm calling an organization that typically responds to calls with a recorded message, by the time the relay operator types the entire message it is often too late to respond and the call is terminated. As an example, this is a slightly edited transcript of the call I made to set up an appointment with an audiologist after deciding that wearing a hearing aid while riding my bicycle might be a pretty good idea. (My comments are not included in the conversation; only the other person's comments are typed by the relay operator.)

Ringing 1 2 (F) (speaker unclear) ent Yes sir hold a on Hello Oh Yes gun on please Yes do me a [HMO identification] number < hold > < give > yeah your name? Okay you have um so you saw Doctor (speaker unclear) Udo 3 you want to come to Kaiser [my HMO] here < you know > you want to come to [name of city]? Oh that is (speaker unclear) let me see who you (speaker unclear) at [name of city] okay alright so you have a referral for audio at least you have 2 referrals and in 1 for audio and 1 for ent OKC you just need audio < ok so > Mm hmm OK I'm coming to you OK we have um we October 8 at 3thirty with Doctor [name of doctor] Mm hmm on a Thursday you want that? The nights we have 11 o'clock 12 1245 I'm going to put you on hold I have to check a patient here okay you want 11 o'clock okay so 11 o'clock on October 9 okay which 1 of the ear do you need the hearing aid for it the last year? Yeah < left ear > that with Doctor (speaker unclear) B. audiogram is with Doctor < the > [name of doctor] you want (speaker unclear) hearing aid which he or is it the last year < ear > < left ear > yes sir okay yeah bye bye.

Fortunately, this was a pretty simple call, so in spite of the typos and unclear comments it didn't take too much guesswork to figure out what was going on. If the subject had been more complicated, then it might not have been successful. In addition, because Kaiser Permanente has an excellent system of electronic records, including appointment schedules, I could immediately go to their Web site, log in, and double check to be sure that my appointment was accurately scheduled, which it was (but with an audiologist, not the doctor referred to in the conversation). A bit inconvenient and not quite perfect? Perhaps, but certainly a useful innovation that makes life less of a hassle for many deaf and hard of hearing people.

Rear Window Captions

Another type of technology worth commenting on is something called rear window captioning, which makes it possible for those of us who have difficulty hearing the dialogue in a movie to follow the conversation, at least in theory. In practice, rear window captioning leaves so much to be desired that in my opinion it is virtually worthless.

To make first-run films accessible for deaf and hard of hearing viewers, many theaters now offer this system, which consists of a dark, semi-transparent piece of Plexiglas about a foot long and four inches wide. This Plexiglas is attached to a flexible, half-inch-thick cable with a base that fits into the soft drink holder on the viewer's seat. By adjusting the cable, the viewer is able to see the captions on the Plexiglas, which are a mirror image of captions shown on the wall near the projector at the back of the theater. It's like the word "ecnalubma" that is printed on the front of some ambulances; the word only becomes clear to the person driving a car and looking in the rear-view mirror.

There are several problems with rear window captioning. For one thing, the letters of the captions at the back of the theater are fairly small, and one has to sit quite far back in the theater for the captions on the Plexiglas to be large enough to read comfortably. Another problem is that there is usually no indication of who is saying what on the captions, so it is sometimes difficult to follow the conversation. In addition, it has been my experience that everything is captioned, which means that one has to spend a lot of time reading, which leaves little time to take in the images on the screen. Sometimes the words on the captions appear and disappear so quickly that it is impossible to read all of them. Also, the Plexiglas needs to be adjusted so that it is slightly below the screen—the

Plexiglas is too dark to see through and the captions are too light to be read unless there is a dark background. Viewers must constantly bob their heads up and down to read the captions and watch the screen. If this wasn't enough, there is sometimes a time lag between what is on the screen and what can be read on the Plexiglas. This lag may only be a few seconds, but it makes it more difficult to follow what's happening. When the lag is fifteen minutes, as was the case in one theater Arlene and I recently visited, it's time to ask for a refund (which we did, and which they were happy to give since they didn't like the system any more than I did). Finally, only a few new films actually have rear window captioning, and these films are primarily action films or family-oriented films. Films of this nature must be very difficult for a young deaf or hard of hearing viewer to follow using this captioning system.

Rear window captioning is, at best, a temporary "solution" to the problem of communication access to feature films. Although many movie theaters, as public accommodations, are required by law to make their facilities accessible, this is not the way to do it. What are some alternatives? One alternative would be to require that all films be captioned, similar to the captioning that one frequently sees on televisions in sports bars or in noisy restaurants, or that many deaf and hard of hearing viewers already use in their homes. When this is used, white captions with a black background run across the bottom or the top of the screen. In practice, these captions can block out a fairly large portion of the screen, and I understand why some people might object to this in a quiet theater. Perhaps with a large screen in a movie theater, the captions could take up a smaller proportion of the screen, but they would still be relatively obtrusive. However, subtitles, like the ones that appear in foreign films, are not very obtrusive. They are different from captions in that there is no stark black background; the subtitles are such that the images on the screen can still easily be seen. If the subtitles can be read easily (if they are large enough and if the color is a good contrast with what's on the screen), then the viewer can comfortably move from reading the subtitles to watching the film without any irritating up and down head movement.* Would a requirement that all films be subtitled add to the cost of a movie ticket? Perhaps, but presumably the rear window captioning system does, too, because that is a system that requires expensive equipment. If subtitles appeared on all films as a matter of course, then the rear window captioning system would not be needed. If one considers the price of popcorn, candy, and soft drinks at movie theaters, adding a few pennies to the price of a ticket to pay for subtitles is mere pocket change.

A rapidly increasing number of films and television programs are available on the Internet, at sites such as Hulu.com and Netflix.com, and many of these films and programs offer subtitles. In general, these subtitles are similar to the subtitles (not the closed captions) that one sees on foreign films in movie theaters. As viewers become used to seeing unobtrusive subtitles on films and television programs on the Internet, perhaps this will help pave the way for a general acceptance of subtitles on first-run films in theaters.

This type of universal access is becoming more popular in other areas as a way to make the world of everyday life more accessible to people with disabilities. Some school systems, for example, such as the one in Maryland where Arlene taught for many years, are beginning to emphasize accessibility for everyone, built into the physical structure and social fabric of the school, rather than having to worry about offering accommodations to individual students on an ad hoc basis. It remains to be seen whether this approach, which includes everything from ramps to the latest forms of technology, will successfully meet the needs of each student.

---

*A good example of this is the film *Sherlock Holmes*, which Arlene and I saw in January 2010. The film was in a theater that had rear window captioning, so I was able to use that technology with some success (but with many of the problems discussed here). A small portion of that film included some subtitles because the dialogue was not in English, and the contrast between the ease of reading the subtitles directly on the screen and the difficulty reading the read-window captions on the Plexiglas below the screen was pronounced. The subtitles were clearer and larger than the captions, and this made it much easier to read and simultaneously watch the images on the screen.

Pediatric Cochlear Implants: A Continuing Controversy

This is not the place for a comprehensive review of the literature related to pediatric cochlear implants.[3] This has been done elsewhere, and interested readers are encouraged to consult some of these books and articles.[4] However, I will offer a few brief observations based primarily on research, some of which I have done (usually with Irene Leigh) and some of which has been done by others. This is a rapidly changing and dynamic area, and many new articles related to cochlear implants appear every month.

One thing that has happened since the beginning of the new millennium is that children are being implanted at younger ages. Even though FDA guidelines have stipulated since 2000 that a child should be at least twelve months old before receiving an implant, there are children, in the United States and abroad, who are implanted long before their first birthday. (Physicians are permitted to override FDA guidelines when they feel it is medically appropriate to do so. In addition, children participating in clinical trials may receive an implant when they are as young as six months.[5]) As an example, the Web site of Children's Memorial Hospital in Chicago (childrensmemorial.org), one of the leading pediatric implant centers in the Midwest, announced that in 2006 a six-month-old infant received bilateral cochlear implants at the center. Although this is still young, it is not unique (outside the United States, some deaf infants have been implanted at even earlier ages), and it is almost certainly a harbinger of things to come.

How many deaf children are receiving implants now? An article in the *Los Angeles Times* (August 3, 2009) estimated that approximately 40 percent of deaf children younger than three years old in the United States now receive either one or two cochlear implants (compared to about 25 percent in 2004, when virtually all of them got only one implant).[6] Assuming this trend continues (the estimates are based on information from the three major cochlear implant companies), it is reasonable to predict that in the near future close to 50 percent of young deaf children, including deaf infants, will receive an implant, and that many of them will receive two. This is still considerably less than the estimated 80 percent of Australian deaf children who receive an implant. (Australia has been at the forefront of cochlear implant research and development for more than three decades, in part because Graeme Clark, one of the true pioneers in the field, is an Australian.)*

Based on information available from the Population Reference Bureau's *2009 World Population Data Sheet* and using the generally accepted assumption that about one deaf child is born for every one thousand live births, I estimate that approximately nine or ten deaf babies are born in the United States each day.[7] Of course, deaf infants are not the only children who get the device; many deaf toddlers and older children are implanted as well. However, the clear trend is to implant younger children, so it seems reasonable to estimate that roughly half of all severely to profoundly deaf kids in the United States will be implanted in the not-too-distant future.

Although it is difficult to accurately estimate the total number of people who have received an implant around the world between the 1980s and 2010, a ballpark figure of 200,000–210,000 (roughly half of

---

*This figure, along with the finding that in Australia some infants as young as two to three months old are being implanted, is reported in Marschark, *Raising and Educating a Deaf Child*. In this context, it is worth noting a recent article in the journal *Audiology and Neurotology*, which reports research conducted in Israel: J. Attias and E. Raveh, "Transient Deafness in Young Candidates for Cochlear Implants," 12 (2007): 325–333. This research suggests that under some conditions infants who are diagnosed as deaf soon after birth may spontaneously recover their hearing, either partially or fully, several months later. Even if this happens only occasionally or even rarely, it would suggest that a decision to implant a child only a few months old may be premature. Even Graeme Clark expressed some reservations about such early implantation in an interview with Patricia Spencer, which appears in Christiansen and Leigh, *Cochlear Implants in Children* (p. 41). Clark said: "I am not sure myself whether it is desirable to operate on [a child] under 12 months." One of his concerns was the need to take the time to ensure that an infant's hearing loss was fully assessed.

whom are children) would be plausible. (On its Web site, the National Information Center on Deafness and Other Communication Disorders estimates 188,000 implantees, worldwide, as of April 2009.) It is not known how many implantees are still using the device, but it is likely that the vast majority are.

~~~

Bilateral implantation is rapidly becoming a popular option for many parents of deaf children. (It is also something that more and more adults are considering.) In a paper presented at the Cochlear Implants and Sign Language Conference at Gallaudet University in spring 2009, Debra Nussbaum, the director of the Cochlear Implant Education Center at the Laurent Clerc National Deaf Education Center, estimated that by the end of 2008 there were at least seven thousand bilateral implant users worldwide and that most of them were children. This number is likely to increase quite rapidly in the future and is most likely more than ten thousand as of December 2010. As one health professional at Johns Hopkins recently told me, "the floodgates are open" for bilateral implantation. There has not been a great deal of research on the effectiveness of bilateral implantation because the phenomenon is still relatively new, but what little there is suggests that children who receive two cochlear implants relatively early in life may do even better, at least in terms of speech perception and identifying the location of sounds, than children who receive one implant.*

Much of the research related to the effectiveness of pediatric implantation since the mid-1980s has focused on speech perception, speech

---

*Anecdotal evidence from conversations I've had with a few adults who use two cochlear implants suggests that having two implants might also make it easier for the user to understand conversations in relatively noisy environments. This was obvious as I was talking to a friend with two implants in a noisy Starbucks. My friend appeared to have a much easier time understanding me than I had understanding her. It remains to be seen whether this is in fact a widespread and consistent benefit from bilateral implantation.

production, and, more recently, the development of language skills. Much of this research has demonstrated that many implanted children do very well in this regard, especially if they have strong parental support, participate in programs that emphasize the development of spoken language, and receive appropriate postimplant auditory training and therapy. Many children with implants also depend on other services, which can range from sign language interpreters to various forms of classroom amplification and real-time captioning.

There is also considerable variation among implanted children in terms of the various outcomes that have been investigated. Some children do better than others in terms of speech and language development, and research continues to sort through the variables or factors that are most important for determining a child's success with the device. If, for example, future research demonstrates that children implanted with two cochlear implants by their first birthday or soon thereafter are more likely to develop speech and language skills on par with—or at least close to—their hearing peers than are those children who receive only one implant (or those who use hearing aids), then this will no doubt accelerate the trend toward bilateral implantation. It is also possible that future bilateral implant users will not need many of the support services that many, if not most, young implant users require today.

Over the years, there has been a fairly significant socioeconomic and racial disparity between deaf children who have received a cochlear implant and those who have not.[8] Families who have good health insurance and are relatively affluent, as well as those who have the experience and expertise (not to mention the time) to deal with intimidating health care bureaucracies, have more access to this technology than those who don't have these resources. This is an important consideration because even one implant costs upward of $40,000. It is likely to continue to be an important issue as the external equipment needs to be replaced. As the story of my ultimately successful effort to replace my old behind-the-ear equipment shows, this might be not something that insurance companies and health maintenance organizations will be eager to pay for, especially if it involves replacing two expensive external devices rather than just one. Although families and implantees are understandably excited about getting one or even two implants, perhaps people also need to carefully consider the extent to which future costs enter the equation and whether a third party will be willing to cover some of those expenses.

—*mm*—

Early communication and language development in young deaf children have always been key issues for parents and teachers. Oliver Sacks, the noted neurologist, emphasizes the importance of early language and communication for deaf children, whether it be sign, speech, or cued speech.* Although Sacks doesn't address cochlear implants in *Seeing Voices* (they were barely on the radar screen in the late 1980s), I suspect he would include them as another possible option as long as they facilitated the development of a child's communication and language abilities.[9] Sacks notes that it is imperative for a child to be exposed to the richest possible language and communication environment, and this exposure should begin as early as possible. In this regard, the emergence of almost universal early infant screening for hearing loss in the United States and elsewhere has greatly reduced late diagnosis, which almost invariably makes it difficult for a deaf child to develop good language and communication skills. During the course of our research in 1999, I heard disheartening stories about insensitive pediatricians and other health professionals who refused to take seriously parents' concerns about their child's inability to hear everyday sounds. In many cases, a definitive diagnosis was not made until the child was more than a year old and sometimes not until the child was two years old. This meant a delay in language and communication development that was difficult to overcome.

---

*Cued speech involves the manipulation of hand shapes and hand placements on and near a speaker's face to produce a visual code representing the sounds, or phonemes, of spoken language.

All parents of deaf children, whether they opt for a cochlear implant or elect to use ASL or some other type of sign communication (or if they do both, as many do), should strongly support early identification of a child's hearing loss so measures can be taken to ensure that the infant has immediate access to language. Even if parents decide to get an implant for their child, it is certainly worth considering some form of sign communication prior to implantation "to provide cognitive and linguistic support for the acquisition of auditory language after cochlear implantation."[10] Moreover, as Marschark points out, there is no evidence that early sign language use interferes with the later development of spoken language. In fact, many parents of children who are not deaf teach their kids some simple signs to make it easier for the children to communicate (asking for milk or water, for example) before they develop an ability to talk.

In the final analysis, cochlear implants are not necessary for a deaf child (or a deaf adult either) to have a rich, rewarding, and successful life, but it is undeniably necessary for all children, deaf and hearing alike, to have good reading, communication, and written language skills. Researchers continue to investigate ways of teaching these skills to deaf children using approaches that focus on visual rather than auditory input. One such project is the Visual Language and Visual Learning (VL2) project at Gallaudet University. The goal of this project "is to gain a greater understanding of the biological, cognitive, linguistic, sociocultural, and pedagogical conditions that influence the acquisition of language and knowledge through the visual modality."[11] Research is occurring in a number of areas under this general rubric, and I hope the VL2 project (as well as other projects and programs) will result in enhanced reading and language development among deaf children who rely primarily on vision to acquire these skills. It is also important for all deaf children, with or without cochlear implants, to develop healthy self-esteem and positive self-image and to interact and communicate effectively with their peers, parents, and older adults.[12]

How do people in the Deaf community feel about cochlear implants, particularly implants for children? This has been a contentious issue since the mid-1980s, and although there is little lingering opposition to implantation among adults, there is still a good bit of resistance to pediatric implantation. This resistance is underscored in a survey that Irene and I conducted at Gallaudet in spring 2008 (and which is discussed in much greater detail in our chapter in *Cochlear Implants and the Deaf Community*). Most of the respondents to this survey (which was very similar to a survey we did in 2000) were undergraduate students, so their responses cannot be taken as representative of the Deaf community as a whole. However, these responses give us an idea of what some deeply committed members of the Deaf community think about cochlear implants these days. Some of the more interesting findings are as follows:

- About 60 percent of the respondents said that it was possible to have a cochlear implant and still have an identity as a Deaf person. This is approximately 10 percent more than in 2000, and it is noteworthy because a much greater proportion of respondents in 2008 were undergraduate students than was the case eight years earlier (80 percent of all respondents in 2008 compared to only 33 percent in 2000). Intuitively, one might surmise that it is unlikely that undergraduate students at Gallaudet would be at the forefront among those in the Deaf community who would agree with this proposition. However, because most of them apparently do, it suggests that other Deaf people are becoming more open to the possibility of someone with a cochlear implant being part of the Deaf community. This is especially true if the person with an implant is comfortable using sign language (as noted in Irene's book, *A Lens on Deaf Identities*).

- About half of the respondents agreed with the statement that Gallaudet University should do more to encourage students with cochlear implants to come to Gallaudet, and even more thought it would be a good idea to have a cochlear implant center at Gallaudet to help meet the needs of Gallaudet students and students in precollege programs on campus (some respondents probably didn't know that there already is such a center).

- Only a quarter of the respondents felt that the Deaf community might disappear because so many children are getting cochlear implants, and about two-thirds said they felt an implant is appropriate for an older person who becomes deaf later in life.
- Although these responses indicate growing acceptance of cochlear implants among at least one segment of the Deaf community, there are indications that this acceptance comes with some qualifications. For one thing, only about 18 percent of those responding to the 2008 survey (compared to 34 percent in 2000) agreed with the statement that faculty and staff should be encouraged to sign with voice whenever possible to make Gallaudet University more "user friendly" for students who use voice communication more than sign, as many cochlear implant users do. This reflects the growing importance of bilingualism on campus, where English and ASL are seen as being separate but equally important languages (as noted earlier, it is not possible to sign in ASL and speak in English word order at the same time). Fluency in both languages is emphasized in a new curriculum that was established in 2007, following the trauma of the 2006 protest on campus. It is reasonable to conclude that if a student with a cochlear implant wants to be a part of the Deaf community, especially at Gallaudet, then fluent signing, preferably sans voice, is likely to be an important consideration. However, this may become less attractive for students with cochlear implants, especially if they are implanted bilaterally at a young age, if their parents and others subsequently focus on the development of spoken language at the expense of learning how to sign, and if the implantees themselves are able to master a spoken language.
- Finally, in both 2000 and 2008, only a little more than one-third of the respondents agreed that hearing parents should be permitted to get a cochlear implant for their child before the age of five if they study the issue carefully and believe this to be the best decision for

the child and the family. This finding probably reflects the views of many Deaf people: implants for adults are one thing, but pediatric implantation is different, and there is still considerable opposition to this in the Deaf community.

In this context, the recent activities of the Deaf Bilingual Coalition (DBC), Audism Free America (AFA), and the National Association of the Deaf (NAD) are important to mention. The mission statement of the DBC, available on its Web site (dbcusa.org), is as follows: "The Deaf Bilingual Coalition promotes the basic human right of all Deaf infants and young children to have access to language and cognitive development through American Sign Language (ASL)." The AFA describes itself as "a grassroots Deaf activist organization . . . which advocates for Deaf American rights, cultural resurgence, and seeks primarily to challenge the ideological foundations of audism in America."* Since their recent conceptions, both organizations have employed a number of confrontational tactics, especially with respect to the Alexander Graham Bell Association for the Deaf and Hard of Hearing (AGB), an organization that advocates for the independence of deaf and hard of hearing people via the development of listening and spoken language skills. Although DBC efforts have not focused primarily on pediatric cochlear implantation, DBC advocates do stress the importance of a strong, visually oriented Deaf community that stands in opposition to the perspective supported by organizations such as AGB. Implicit in the DBC's message is that there is no need for pediatric implants as long as deaf children are exposed to a vibrant Deaf community and a vibrant, visual language such as ASL.

---

*AFA defines *audism* as "attitudes and practices based on the assumption that behaving in the ways of those who speak and hear is desired and best. It produces a system of privilege, thus resulting in stigma, bias, discrimination, and prejudice—in overt or covert ways—against Deaf culture, American Sign Language, and Deaf people of all walks of life." See audismfreeamerica .blogspot.com.

As far as the more formally organized, 130-year-old NAD is concerned, information about implants on this organization's Web site (nad. org) is limited but does include the NAD's 2000 position paper on cochlear implants, mentioned earlier, as well as a few links to other resources. In general, it appears that at the present time issues related to cochlear implantation are not very high on the NAD's list of priorities. Whether this simply represents a growing acceptance of a form of technology that a rapidly increasing number of deaf children and adults are using or whether it simply means that the NAD has formally or informally decided to allow the issue to evolve on its own is difficult to determine.

In sum, in contrast to the situation at the beginning of the twenty-first century, cochlear implantation has moved away from the forefront of attention among many people in the Deaf community. However, this does not indicate an unqualified acceptance of implants among a large segment of the Deaf population. There is still opposition to pediatric implants, especially among those who identify strongly with the Deaf community as well as those who are generally opposed to surgery on an otherwise healthy person for ethical reasons. In addition, recently formed organizations such as AFA are attempting to resurrect opposition to pediatric implantation within the framework of audism, the presumed denigration of ASL, and renewed concerns about the actual benefits of cochlear implantation.

Notes

1. John B. Christiansen and Irene W. Leigh, *Cochlear Implants in Children: Ethics and Choices* (Washington, D.C.: Gallaudet University Press, 2002/2005).

2. John B. Christiansen and Sharon N. Barnartt, *Deaf President Now! The 1988 Revolution at Gallaudet University* (Washington, D.C.: Gallaudet University Press, 1995).

3. Some of the information in this section is taken or adapted from John B. Christiansen and Irene W. Leigh, "Cochlear Implants and Deaf Community Perceptions," in *Cochlear Implants and the Deaf Community*, ed. Raylene Paludneviciene and

Irene W. Leigh (Washington, D.C.: Gallaudet University Press, forthcoming). Irene's contributions are gratefully acknowledged, although she should not be held accountable for any of the personal views or opinions I express in this section.

4. See Kate A. Belzner and Brenda C. Seal, "Children with Cochlear Implants: A Review of Demographics and Communication Outcomes," *American Annals of the Deaf* 154, no. 3 (2009): 311–333; Marc Marschark, *Raising and Educating a Deaf Child*, 2nd ed. (New York: Oxford University Press, 2007); Christiansen and Leigh, *Cochlear Implants in Children*; Patricia Elizabeth Spencer and Marc Marschark, "Cochlear Implants: Issues and Implications," in *Oxford Handbook of Deaf Studies, Language, and Education*, ed. M. Marschark and P. E. Spencer (New York: Oxford University Press, 2005); and dozens of articles from journals such as *Ear and Hearing, Journal of Deaf Studies and Deaf Education, Sign Language Studies, Volta Review, Journal of Speech, Language, and Hearing Research, American Annals of the Deaf*, and *Archives of Otolaryngology—Head and Neck Surgery*.

5. Marschark, *Raising and Educating a Deaf Child*, p. 47.

6. Shari Roan, "Cochlear Implants Open Deaf Kids' Ears to the World," *Los Angeles Times*, August 3, 2009.

7. See Christiansen and Leigh, "Cochlear Implants and Deaf Community Perceptions," in Paludneviciene and Leigh, *Cochlear Implants and the Deaf Community*, for a discussion of this computation.

8. See Christiansen and Leigh, *Cochlear Implants in Children*, and Belzner and Seal, "Children with Cochlear Implants."

9. Oliver Sacks, *Seeing Voices: A Journey into the World of the Deaf* (Berkeley: University of California Press, 1989).

10. Marschark, *Raising and Educating a Deaf Child*, p. 51.

11. See http://vl2.gallaudet.edu.

12. For issues such as these, I recommend Irene W. Leigh's book, *A Lens on Deaf Identities* (New York: Oxford University Press, 2009).

Part III.

The 2006 Protest at Gallaudet University

The Search

ON MAY 1, 2006, the Gallaudet University Board of Trustees announced that Jane K. Fernandes, the university's provost, had been chosen as the ninth president of the university. Dr. Fernandes's appointment was not popular among a large segment of the Gallaudet community (or among many people in the larger Deaf community). Her selection led to a prolonged, emotionally charged protest that began a few minutes after the announcement was made, continued for a few weeks in May, was suspended during the summer, and resumed again in October. After several additional weeks of intensive and relentless opposition in the fall, the protesters persuaded the Board of Trustees to rescind Fernandes's appointment, even though the board had unanimously selected her only a few months earlier.

A version of this chapter appeared as "The 2006 Protest at Gallaudet University: Reflections and Explanations," *Sign Language Studies* 10, no. 1 (2009): 69–89.

Given that Fernandes was chosen as Gallaudet's president after a lengthy and comprehensive search process, why did so many people react negatively to her appointment? Why did many people believe she was unqualified to serve as the university's president? And, given that this was the second major protest related to a presidential search at the university in less than twenty years, what is there about Gallaudet that seems to encourage an unconventional or confrontational response as the first rather than last step?

I cannot objectively analyze the events of 2006 on Gallaudet's campus because I was a member of the search committee that recommended Fernandes, along with two other candidates, to the Board of Trustees. Consequently, in this chapter, I will offer some personal observations about what happened and why.

―*⁓⁓*―

At the beginning of the fall semester of 2005, Gallaudet's president, I. King Jordan, announced that he would be retiring at the end of 2006. Dr. Jordan's tenure had begun in March 1988, after the historic events of Deaf President Now (DPN) had captured the imagination of people, deaf and hearing alike, throughout the world. A few weeks after President Jordan informed the campus community of his intentions, the Board of Trustees announced that it would be forming a search committee to lead the effort to find a new president for Gallaudet. Four faculty representatives would be on this seventeen-member committee, and several of my colleagues urged me to become a part of the group. After mulling over the matter for a few days, I decided that, if selected, I would serve. Little did I realize what was in store for me—or for the university, for that matter.

Since many other people on the faculty were also interested in serving, the faculty committee responsible for elections set up a special election in October so that eight faculty members could be recommended to the board for service on the committee. The faculty did not directly elect the faculty representatives; rather, eight names were submitted by faculty officers to the board, and the board, seeking diversity, selected four of them. As it happened, my name was included among those that the faculty officers sent to the board.

At the time, I was pretty sure that I would not be chosen. As a white person, a male, and a nonnative user of ASL, I thought the board would probably pick others for the committee. I did not think the fact that I had a cochlear implant would work in my favor, either. However, for whatever reason, the board selected me as one of the faculty representatives, and I was excited about what would be my last experience on a search committee at Gallaudet. I had served on several such committees before, including two searches for deans, and thought I had a good idea of what to expect. As they say, I didn't know the half of it.

The vast majority of search committee members introduced to the campus in early November were deaf or hard of hearing, and many were people of color. The group included two representatives from the professional staff, two alumni, one undergraduate student, one graduate student, six Board of Trustee members, a representative from the university's precollege programs (the Laurent Clerc National Deaf Education Center), and four faculty. Soon after members were chosen for the committee, we selected a consulting firm, Academic Search, Inc.—a Washington, D.C., organization with extensive experience in college and university presidential searches—to assist us in our effort.

The position was formally announced in mid-February, and we gave candidates about six weeks to apply, informing aspirants that "materials received by the end of March [would] be assured of full consideration." The committee cast a very wide net, asking people on campus and others in the Deaf community for nominations and recommendations, holding open forums, and advertising the position on Gallaudet's Web site and many other online venues. Our consultants, doing what consultants typically do in university presidential searches, also spent a great deal of time actively recruiting qualified candidates. We wanted to complete the process by early May 2006 so that an announcement could be made before students and faculty left campus for the summer. It would not have been acceptable to the campus community to have the board announce the result during the summer, and many people felt that waiting until the fall was not a good idea, either.

The long and tedious process of sifting through the résumés, letters of recommendation, and supporting material took up much of late March and early April. As in virtually every search of this nature, the committee thoroughly discussed the candidates' strengths and weaknesses; eventually, six people were invited to have formal interviews with the search committee in April at an off-campus location (to preserve confidentiality).

It would be inappropriate, unethical, and probably illegal to describe what led to the selection of these six individuals, but the committee spent a tremendous amount of time and energy to ensure that each candidate was given serious consideration for inclusion in this select group. Clearly, issues of diversity, educational background, and experience were on my mind (and presumably everyone else's). Given the relatively large size of the search committee, there was not always unanimity about whom to invite for an interview. However, after lengthy discussions, a formal vote was taken to determine which candidates should be given further consideration. The six semifinalists were all deaf and included women and at least one person of color.

Following these six off-campus interviews, the committee selected three candidates as the finalists for the position: Ronald Stern, Stephen Weiner, and Jane Fernandes. At the time, Stern was the superintendent of the New Mexico School for the Deaf, Weiner was a professor and former dean at Gallaudet, and Fernandes was Gallaudet's provost.

The Three Finalists

As the search committee's work was winding down, the sense of anticipation and tension on campus was increasing. This became apparent when the criticisms began shortly after the names of the three finalists were announced. One objection was that Ron Stern did not have a terminal degree (usually defined as a PhD or EdD).[1] However, he did have detailed plans to complete his degree by the time he assumed the position if he were chosen. Another major criticism was more disturbing to me and perhaps to many of the other search committee members: that the search committee did not sufficiently consider candidates of color. This was apparently obvious to many people on campus because all of the finalists were white.

Various organizations on campus, including the university faculty, focused on this matter and issued various pronouncements. After one general faculty meeting, shortly after the three finalists were announced, a member of the faculty (who was not a member of the search committee) e-mailed me to say it was appalling and absurd for members of the search committee, many of whom were persons of color, to be criticized for the absence of racial diversity among the three finalists. Unfortunately, my faculty colleague did not share this perception in the meeting. I found some of the comments made in the faculty meeting to be hurtful and even ludicrous, considering all the work the committee had done (as well as our oft-stated commitment to diversity), but I didn't feel it was appropriate to become too involved publicly in defending our efforts. Members of the committee had pledged to keep our work confidential, and consequently we were reluctant to say too much, whether in large forums or in small discussions with our colleagues. I also felt that because the search was as fair and transparent as anyone could reasonably expect, people should at least be willing to grudgingly accept our decision to recommend these three candidates, even if they disagreed.

There is an inevitable tension between the need to keep some information confidential in a university presidential search and, at the same time, share as much information as possible with the campus community. For example, some candidates might not want their current employer to know that they are searching for a new position, and writers of letters of recommendation typically assume that their letters will not be shared with the candidate or anyone else outside the formal search process. At the same time, interested constituencies, including faculty, staff, and students, are understandably eager to be kept informed of search committee activities and progress. There is no easy way to resolve this tension, but frequent and regular communication with the campus community by the chair of the search committee, which most assuredly *did* occur in this search, is important. It is also important for those in the larger campus community to trust those on a search committee to do the job they were elected or appointed to do.

On April 24, by a "clear majority" the faculty senate (an elected group of about twenty faculty representatives primarily responsible for faculty governance matters such as the curriculum and peer-review policies) approved a resolution that noted that "none of the final three candidates are of racially diverse backgrounds" and asked the Board of Trustees to postpone the selection of the president until the fall. The resolution also asked the board to "ADD persons of diverse racial and ethnic backgrounds to the existing final pool of candidates."

That same day, the leaders of the Coalition of Organizations for Students of Color at Gallaudet sent an open letter to the Board of Trustees, which had been "drafted by a coalition of deaf people of color, including students, alumni, faculty, staff, administrators and friends."[2] This letter called the search process into question, primarily because "a candidate of color who possesses all of the qualifications [for the position] was overlooked." Because of this, the letter accused the search committee and the board of creating a "hostile environment."

In another April 24 letter, this one addressed to the search committee, the Board of Trustees, and the Gallaudet community, six members of the Professional Education Programs Diversity and Field Placement Committee also addressed these matters.* They suggested that the absence

---

*This is a unit within the graduate school at Gallaudet that is primarily responsible for monitoring the quality of the university's teacher education programs, as well as other school and education-related programs.

of a person of color among the three finalists called into question "the genuineness of the university's commitment to multiculturalism and especially the goal of actively recruiting qualified candidates of color for positions at Gallaudet." According to the authors, "this particular outcome may even contribute to the perpetuation of institutional racism within our university community." Later in the letter, they suggested that their criticisms had less to do with the three finalists and more to do with the "overall presidential search *process*. We believe the selection of the search committee itself and of the final candidates has lacked *transparency* and *equity*." (All italics are in the original letter.)

All of these letters contain some serious charges. Issues of white and hearing privilege (that is, racism and audism) undoubtably pervade our society and, at times, Gallaudet University itself. Like many organizations, the university needs to do more to confront and effectively deal with these issues. Perhaps, though, one reason for the outrage expressed in these letters is that in the months and years leading up to April 2006, the university had been making headway in dealing with cultural diversity. As the Professional Education Programs Diversity and Field Placement Committee authors noted, "For the past year and a half, the university has invested considerable time and energy into addressing issues of cultural diversity and equity throughout our educational community—even to the extent of adding a university wide initiative dedicated to diversity." Perhaps partly because of this initiative, many people expected that a person of color would be selected as the president of the university or at least make it into the final group. Thus, when these expectations were not met, a great deal of anger and disappointment ensued.

Although these concerns are serious, the sweeping condemnations of the search committee and the Board of Trustees, primarily because a person of color was not included among the three finalists, are not warranted. The fact that one African American candidate (who was actually named in the April 24 letter written by the Professional Education Programs Diversity and Field Placement Committee) was considered but not included among the finalists apparently made little difference to those who wrote these letters.

Because of confidentiality issues, members of the search committee cannot explain publicly why any specific candidate did not make it to the next round in the selection process. If the process were to be that transparent, as some have suggested, this would violate all of the norms of how search committees, whether at educational institutions or other organizations, should operate. Few people would be willing to apply for a position in such an environment. Moreover, the charge that the "selection of the search committee itself . . . lacked *transparency* and *equity*" is equally nonsensical, given that this process was widely shared with the campus community, virtually all campus constituencies participated in the selection process, and extensive efforts were made at all levels to ensure that the committee reflected the diversity of the Gallaudet community.

Given the persistent criticism of the presidential search committee in 2006, especially the widespread comment that there was a "lack of adequate diversity in the finalists" (in the words of one faculty leader of the protest who posted a letter on deafdc.com), it is interesting that this criticism was absent in the subsequent presidential search, in 2009, at Gallaudet. The 2009 search was conducted to replace Robert Davila, who served as the president of the university from January 2007 to December 2009. As was the case in 2006, the 2009 search was fair and transparent, and the four finalists were applauded (on various blogs and elsewhere) for their commitment to Deaf culture and for their qualifications. Like the finalists in 2006, the finalists in 2009 were all white. However, unlike 2006, there were almost no comments or criticisms (on blogs or elsewhere) related to the lack of diversity among the finalists in 2009. Although there may be a number of reasons for this, it is likely that few people on campus wanted to revisit the issues that were so divisive three years earlier and did not want to risk jeopardizing the university's standing in the academic community. As will be discussed later, this standing was called into question after the 2006 protest.

The New President

The three finalists made their much-anticipated presentations to the campus community during the last two weeks of April. Steve Weiner spoke first, early in the week of April 17. Ron Stern presented later that week, and Jane Fernandes gave her speech in the middle of the following week. The scheduling was criticized by some because it seemed to give Fernandes an advantage in that she would have more time to prepare. She would also know what the other two candidates had said, if she were inclined to pay attention to their presentations. Moreover, because she was already the provost and had presumably thought more than the other two about the question we wanted the candidates to discuss, why give her more time? Logically, the outsider, Ron Stern, should have had more time to prepare than either of the two campus locals.

I agree that this was not an ideal situation. It would have been better if the candidates had made their presentations back-to-back on three consecutive days. However, there were serious scheduling problems, and given the severe time constraints at the end of the process, this was the best arrangement that could be made. Moreover, because the scheduling was handled by someone with close ties to the president's office, it unfortunately gave the impression that that office and perhaps King Jordan himself were involved.

A task force established by the Board of Trustees in fall 2007 to review the presidential search cites this issue as the single most important perceived flaw in the search process. On the basis of surveys conducted among various constituencies, the task force noted the "overwhelming concern about the President's Office conducting improper interference with the presidential search process as the President's office staff had much greater access to the PSC [presidential search committee] than others on campus. . . . The inclusion of a President's Office staff member in PSC meetings, her doing background checks on the search firms and candidates, and the President's direct communication with PSC members and final candidates were all seen as inappropriate."

In spite of the task force's conclusion, there was no "direct communication" between President Jordan and the members of the search committee. I certainly had no communication, direct or indirect, with him, with the possible exception of attending his annual end-of-the-year holiday reception in December. Nevertheless, many people perceived that there was too much involvement by the president and his office, which made it easier for some of them to conclude that entire search process was rigged and unfair.

This is another example of the "definition of the situation," mentioned earlier, which emphasizes the importance of beliefs and perceptions in defining reality and the consequences of such definitions. Over the years, sociologists have come up with a variety of different ways to express this core idea. One of my favorite conceptualizations was made by Roy Francis, a professor at the University of Wisconsin, Milwaukee: "If something is believed to be true, it is true in its consequences."[3] It often doesn't matter if something is really true as long as a significant number of people believe it to be true. For example, a large number of people believe, against all geological evidence, that the world was created in six days and is only about ten thousand years old. Even though this is demonstrably not the case, for those who believe it is true and act accordingly, the facts are not allowed to get in the way of belief.

━━━

For the presentations, we asked the candidates to focus on their vision for the university during the next five to seven years. We also asked them to limit their formal comments to about twenty minutes, thereby leaving plenty of time for questions. Because Weiner and Stern had only a few days or at most a week to prepare, whereas Fernandes had almost two weeks, it was difficult to compare them on their presentation skills. Weiner's presentation, for example, lasted about forty minutes, and Stern significantly exceeded the twenty-minute limit as well. Even though their presentations were long, both were reasonably clear, covered the topic well, and had inspiring moments. In addition, both Stern and Weiner responded thoughtfully to the questions they received. Fernandes's presentation, on the other hand, while more formal and perhaps less inspirational than the other two, nevertheless adequately covered the topic in about twenty minutes. This was fortunate because it left a lot of time for questions, and she got plenty of them, many of which were challenging and even quite hostile. Nonetheless, she rose to the occasion, didn't lose her cool, and responded professionally to her interlocutors.

At the conclusion of each presentation, the attendees were asked to fill out evaluation forms, which were collected and shared with the search committee. There were hundreds of completed forms for each candidate, which made for long hours of reading for search committee members.

―*ᜭᜭᜭ*―

After the three presentations, the committee met one last time, discussed everything we had learned about the candidates, and made our recommendations to the Gallaudet Board of Trustees. The board, like governing boards at most other universities, is ultimately responsible for selecting the president of the university. We were not charged with ranking the candidates; instead, we shared our perceptions of each one's strengths and weaknesses. This was done in writing, but the committee also met with the board to answer any questions it had. Because six members of the board were already on the search committee, if other board members had additional questions about what had happened during the search process, these six members could presumably share that information with them. Following our meeting, the Board of Trustees interviewed each candidate at length during the last weekend in April.

On Monday, May 1, shortly before the campus was informed of the board's selection, the search committee met briefly with one of the board members who was also a member of the search committee. In that meeting, we were informed that Jane Fernandes was the board's unanimous choice. Immediately after that meeting, we were led to the auditorium where, in reserved seats, we joined hundreds of others who were eager to hear the news.

The Immediate Reaction

The news from the Board of Trustee interim chair, Celia May Baldwin, that Fernandes was the board's unanimous selection as the ninth president of the university was not universally applauded, to say the least. Many people were visibly upset, some walked out in anger, and Ryan Commerson, a graduate student, soon headed to the front of the auditorium to interrupt the proceedings and announce that the decision would be challenged.* Officers from campus security were nearby (clearly indicating that at least some people were aware that a disturbance might develop) and quickly hustled him away. People congregated outside, and the *Washington Post* reported on the front page the next day that "within moments of the announcement, a mass of students had blocked the main gates of the campus in Northeast Washington."[4] The "mass" was composed of not only students but faculty, staff, and alumni as well.

Over the next two weeks, a tent city, complete with wi-fi, television sets, and cooking equipment, sprang up near the university's main entrance, ad hoc organizational structures were established, and numerous rallies, news conferences, forums, and meetings took place. Some forums involved Board of Trustee members and protesters, with the former trying unsuccessfully to persuade the latter to accept the board's deci-

---

*In this action, Commerson, whether intentionally or not, was emulating Harvey Goodstein, a Gallaudet faculty member. In 1988, Goodstein stepped in front of the then-chair of the Board of Trustees who was attempting to defend the board's choice of Elisabeth Zinser in a large gathering in the university's field house. Like Commerson, Goodstein had encouraged the audience not to accept the board's decision and to demonstrate its opposition. Ironically, in 2006, Goodstein, having retired from the faculty, was a member of Gallaudet's Board of Trustees, the body that selected Jane Fernandes.

Protesters near Gallaudet's front entrance on May 1, 2006, shortly after the announcement of Jane Fernandes's selection as the ninth president of the university (Gallaudet University Office of Public Relations; no photographer identified).

sion. Perhaps the most important new ad hoc group that emerged was the Faculty, Staff, Students, and Alumni (FSSA) coalition, a group that quickly established a Web site, appointed a media contact representative, and in other ways coordinated protest-related activities. Other Web sites and blogs were active as well, including deafdc.com, gallynet.org, and deafhotnews.net, and contributions easily could be made online to support the protest.

For approximately two weeks after Fernandes's selection, members of the university faculty also weighed in with letters, memos, and occasional formal and informal meetings. One day after the announcement, the Professional Education Programs faculty (some of whom, as noted earlier, had written a letter focusing on the lack of diversity among the three finalists) wrote a memorandum to the Board of Trustees, the search committee, and the university community. In this memo, they "respectfully request[ed]" that Jane Fernandes "step down" as president of the university and "that a new search process be conducted." (Of course, Fernandes was not yet Gallaudet's president; King Jordan was not scheduled to retire until December 31.)

About a week after the announcement, the university faculty formally voted on five resolutions: First, a resolution in support of the board's decision to appoint Jane Fernandes failed to pass. Then, four resolutions passed: one requesting that Fernandes "publicly renounce her appointment," another calling for a reopening of the search, a third expressing no confidence in "Dr. Jane Fernandes as president-elect," and a final one expressing no confidence in the decision of the Board of Trustees to appoint Fernandes.

It is instructive to compare the votes at this meeting with similar faculty votes during the DPN protest in March 1988. This protest began soon after the Gallaudet University Board of Trustees announced that a hearing woman, Elisabeth Zinser, had been selected from among three finalists as the seventh president of the university. The other two finalists were deaf men, and the major issue that precipitated the protest was that, after 124 years as a federally chartered institution, many people felt a deaf person should be the president of Gallaudet. As was the case 18 years later, meetings and rallies were held during DPN, and the faculty voted on several resolutions while the protest was in full swing. One important difference between DPN and the protest in 2006 was that DPN was a one- or two-week event, whereas the latter took place over five or six weeks in May and October.

In the faculty meeting on May 8, 2006, Jane Fernandes was supported by approximately one-third of the faculty in the first resolution, and in the second resolution, 47 percent—almost half—voted against the resolution asking her to renounce her appointment. (The other resolutions were supported by 60 to 70 percent of the faculty.) Even though the resolutions passed in 1988 were different in emphasis from those approved in 2006 (asking for the resignation of different people, for example), they garnered much more faculty support than was the case eighteen years later. One resolution in 1988 calling for the resignation of the chair of the Board of Trustees was supported by almost 97 percent of the faculty. Other resolutions were passed by similarly lopsided majorities in 1988. Although one faculty protest leader in 2006 was quoted in the *Washington Post* in early May as saying that "99.9 percent of the people here support this protest,"[5] this was clearly not the case among the faculty at that time. In mid-October, when the faculty formally addressed the matter again, the votes against Fernandes and the board more closely resembled the large majorities seen in 1988 (garnering majorities of 80 to 90 percent, except for a vote of no confidence in King Jordan, which was narrowly approved). By that time, even many faculty members who had originally supported Fernandes in May were resigned to the fact that she likely would not be able to function as the university's president.

Although many faculty members supported the general goals of the protest, some clearly did not, and some students didn't either. Jane Norman, a Deaf professor in the Department of Communication Studies, wrote an "open letter to the community" on May 4: "It must be made known that not all faculty . . . staff and students support the protest. . . . Many of us are being pressured to join the protest. . . . We have the right to support Dr. Jane Fernandes. This does not mean that we do not hold ASL and Deaf culture dear to our hearts. . . . Dr. Jane Fernandes has worked long and hard on diversity. . . . We are focusing on diversity. Gallaudet is struggling to become a place for all Deaf people." A few days after Dr. Norman's letter appeared, a nine-page listing of "Responses to Jane Norman's Open Letter to the Community" was distributed by the university administration. These responses, including some responses from students, strongly endorsed Norman's position and showed that a sizeable number of people did not support the protest.

—*mm*—

There was no resolution to the conflict by mid-May, and after the commencement exercises, people started leaving campus for the summer. Among other things, Baldwin resigned as chair of the Board of Trustees, citing "numerous aggressive threats," and Fernandes resigned as provost to focus on the transition to her presidency and otherwise spend time trying to convince the campus community that she was the right person for the position. Even though the tent city shut down after commencement, many of the protesters were not finished; as one said, "We'll see you in the fall."

People maintained Web sites throughout the summer so others could keep in touch, and "Unity for Gallaudet" T-shirts were sold at the National Association of the Deaf (NAD) convention in late June and early July. This slogan had been written by those who opposed Fernandes's selection. These shirts, as well as other T-shirts with the phrase "Know Thy Enemy" and sporting an unflattering image of Fernandes, were worn by many protesters and sympathizers during the protest—and long after the protest was over.

In late June, President Jordan issued new "Guidelines for Expressive Activities and Assemblies" that spelled out revised policies for allowing protests and other forms of expression on campus. These policies were thought to be necessary after the disruptions that had taken place on campus in May. Although Jordan explained that these policies were designed to make it possible for people to disagree peacefully, would not interfere with the right of free expression, and were similar to guidelines at other universities, his actions were interpreted by many supporters of the protest as stifling dissent. As one letter from the FSSA coalition to the campus community said, the new guidelines "are an example of current administration attempts to control and rule this campus by oppression, intimidation, and fear." Also during the summer, the FSSA coalition produced a twelve-page brochure entitled "Unity for Gallaudet: We Stand for Justice." This glossy, multicolored brochure described the work of FSSA, portrayed the protest in terms of a quest for social justice, and stated that the coalition "demands a new search that is inclusive, fair, and free from interference and manipulation."

A Few Months Later . . .

Things picked up again in late September and early October as the fall meeting of Gallaudet's Board of Trustees approached. Many of those opposed to Fernandes's selection saw this as their last chance to convince the board to change its mind, since Jordan was scheduled to leave office at the end of December. The tent city was set up again; various letters, press releases, and position papers were written and disseminated to the campus community (by those opposed to Fernandes as well as those who supported her selection); meetings were held; and the protest's emotional level increased by several orders of magnitude over what it

The tent city, October 15, 2006 (Gallaudet Office of Public Relations; photograph by Ralph Fernandez).

had been five months earlier. This was reflected in some of the other events that occurred in October: a hunger strike and candlelight vigil, organized walkouts from classes, destruction of property, bomb threats, disruption of gatherings honoring King Jordan and his wife, occupations of university buildings, the postponement of homecoming (many events, including the football game, were moved off campus), denials of access to the university, class cancellations (including those at the high school and elementary school on campus), counterprotests (some students and professors tried to hold classes outside), initial responses from the Board of Trustees stating that it would not change its decision, and, perhaps the most traumatic of all, the arrest of more than 130 protesters on Friday, October 13.

The Protesters and King Jordan

Anger at and resentment of King Jordan was an important subtext throughout the protest in 2006. Although Jordan enjoyed almost universal acclaim when he was selected as the university's president in 1988, over the years he gradually lost support from a number of quarters. For example, in 2000 he was roundly criticized by the faculty for his appointment of Jane Fernandes as provost without going through a normal search process. (Not surprisingly, the circumstances of this appointment, as well as Jordan's unwavering and uncritical support of Fernandes over the years, were frequently brought up in 2006 as another reason to reject Fernandes as Gallaudet's president.) Moreover, even though Jordan was a prolific fundraiser who enjoyed widespread support among members of Congress, he and others in his administration were criticized by some on campus for not effectively dealing with important issues such as declining student enrollment and the perceived erosion of academic standards.[6]

Even though there was growing disenchantment with Jordan, which included allegations of inappropriately influencing the selection of Fernandes in the spring, nothing prepared the campus for the tumultuous events that began on Thursday, October 5. Early that afternoon, Linda Jordan, King Jordan's wife, was honored for her long-standing support of the arts at the university at the newly renamed Linda K. Jordan Gallery in the Washburn Arts Building. The *Washington Post* described the events: "Yesterday, students waved cardboard coffins and signs and marched to a ceremony naming a gallery for Linda Jordan. They were yelling so loudly, said some who couldn't get through the crowd, that deaf people outside could feel the vibrations in the glass windows. Someone threw water or juice into the crowd."[7]

Later that afternoon, the raucous protest continued at the Student Academic Center, which was being renamed in King Jordan's honor (Jordan's name was actually chiseled off an outside wall by one of the protesters), and at a dinner to honor the Jordans that evening in the Kellogg Conference Center hosted by the Board of Trustees. Protesters convened outside this invitation-only event and attempted to disrupt it by pounding on the windows. At the end of the evening, guests were escorted out of the back of the conference center by campus security officers.

Another group of protesters occupied Hall Memorial Building, one of the main academic buildings on campus, late Thursday night. This occupation lasted several days.

During the week of October 9, the protesters disrupted classes and effectively shut down the university. King Jordan repeatedly warned the student body that arrests would occur unless the campus was reopened. In a midweek statement to the campus community, Jordan wrote: "This illegal and unlawful behavior must stop. The faculty members who are instigating and manipulating the students have simply gone too far in pursuit of their own agendas. If there is a confrontation, the dissenters will have caused it. They must take full responsibility for the consequences of their actions, including possible arrest and suspension."

On Wednesday, October 11, the FSSA coalition issued a press release that stated, in part, that "today, students declared a 'Coup d' Universite' and said they no longer recognized Dr. I. King Jordan as President of the University." The press release also described the important role of Gallaudet's football team in changing the nature of the protest: "40 members of the 60 member football team, along with many of their student supporters, marched through campus, locking gates, and blocking entrances at approximately 3:00 Wednesday morning." The press release said that the reason a number of football players decided to join the protest was that they were concerned about the "lack of successful retention of team members" and that they were unwilling "to live in an oppressive, fearful environment any longer."

Friday the 13th

The campus was not reopened by the end of the week, and shortly after 9:00 p.m. on Friday, October 13, in full view of television cameras and police spotlights, police began making arrests. According to sociology professor Margaret Vitullo, who was on the scene as an observer, the police arrested only those protesters who were actually sitting in the road. Anyone who was standing off to the side, or who got up and walked off the street, was not arrested. The next day, a front-page article in the *Washington Post* quoted Jordan as saying, "I deeply regret being forced to take this action. . . . But the protesters have left me no choice."[8] The article describes the events after Jordan made his decision: "Teams of officers, acting on orders from President I. King Jordan, and aided by interpreters in orange vests, picked up individual students, who went limp, and carried them to a D.C. police van." Not only students were arrested for unlawful assembly, however: also included were leaders of DPN, such as Tim Rarus, who had worked hard to elevate Jordan to the Gallaudet presidency eighteen years earlier. Rarus was quoted as saying: "I helped put you in office, now you're arresting me!"[9] In this same *Washington Post* article, Jordan reportedly said that the decision to go ahead with the arrests was the most difficult decision of his presidency: "I know in my heart it was the right decision . . . but my heart's really pained." The next day, Jordan further justified his decision by saying it resulted "from a 'complete lack of good faith' on the part of the protesters."[10]

In spite of ongoing disruptions, the arrests, and the growing sentiment expressed by many people, on and off campus, that it would be difficult, if not impossible, for Fernandes to assume the presidency in the current climate, the Board of Trustees continued to insist that it

Protesters at front entrance of the university
(Photograph by Barbara White. Used with permission).

would not change its mind and stood behind its May decision to appoint Fernandes. Mark Weinberg, the chair of the university faculty, said: "Regardless of her abilities, it's obvious that the institution can't continue under the leadership of Jane Fernandes. There's too much opposition to her."[11] In a memo to the campus community two days after the arrests (October 15), the new chair of the board, Brenda Jo Brueggemann, wrote: "Our decision to support Dr. Jane K. Fernandes as the ninth president of Gallaudet University stands. . . . We conducted a fair, open and transparent search for a new president and we selected Dr. Fernandes as the strongest candidate. . . . The Board will not remove Dr. Fernandes from a position she has not yet started."*

---

*During the protest at Gallaudet, various groups around the country gathered to support what the protesters were trying to accomplish in Washington, D.C. In one incident (which should not be taken as typical) approximately fifteen protesters in Ohio demonstrated their displeasure with the board's decision by staging a sit-in outside Brueggemann's office at Ohio State University, where she is a member of the faculty. There was also bomb threat in the same building.

A week after the occupation of Hall Memorial Building began, the Board of Trustees hired a prestigious Washington, D.C., law firm, Covington and Burling, to investigate and issue a report, a document that was released in January 2007. This report, entitled *Report of Investigation: Gallaudet University Events at Hall Memorial Building on October 6, 2006*, was based on a review of relevant documents and videotapes, as well as a number of interviews with students and members of the campus police force. The report, written by a team headed by Eric H. Holder Jr. (later the attorney general of the United States), included the following points:

1. After attempting to disrupt the dinner honoring the Jordans, many protesters convened in the Student Union to discuss what to do next because they had concluded that the Board of Trustees was unwilling to change its decision. As the report notes: "A consensus developed in favor of entering and occupying a campus building in an effort to 'make [the Board] understand' and 'listen.'" The takeover of Hall Memorial Building began about 10:30 p.m. on October 5, and "the building quickly filled up during the ensuing hours" (p. 12).

2. About seven o'clock the following morning, a bomb threat was called in to the Department of Public Safety headquarters on campus. The report notes that, contrary to what some people argued at the time, there is indisputable evidence that a bomb threat was actually called in (using voice telephone, not a TTY), and that the "primary objective" of the three officers who were dispatched to Hall Memorial Building was to search the building to see if there was a bomb there. Although this was the primary objective, the report concludes that it was not the only one: The person who called in the threat did not specifically say that the bomb was in Hall Memorial Building, but the Department of Public Safety focused its attention on that building "with an eye toward putting an end to the occupation" (p. 6). At the same time, the authors of the report concluded that there

continued

was, in their words, "no evidence" that someone from the university administration called in the bomb threat as a pretext for gaining access to the building.

3. After the Department of Public Safety investigated the bomb threat, three members of the department were accused of using excessive force during this investigation. In fact, the primary reason the Board of Trustees hired Covington and Burling to investigate the events in Hall Memorial Building was to determine whether this charge was valid.

4. The Covington and Burling report states that "students aggressively resisted the officers' entry, viewing the officers as intruders and fearing that they would seek to eject the protesters from the building" (p. 5). In addition, "officers and students whom we interviewed told us that the protesters formed rows of 'human chains' (people standing together with locked arms) in an attempt to prevent the officers from moving further into the building. A videotape of this portion of the incident shows dozens of students yelling at the officers, blocking the officers' forward progress and, at times, moving toward the officers" (p. 19).

5. Soon after the officers gained access to Hall Memorial Building, one of them became separated from the other two and, as the report notes, "as this officer moved through the building, students followed him, initiating physical contact on their own by pushing him, cutting in front of him suddenly and holding their ground, and also shouting at and otherwise provoking him. In one fast-paced set of interactions on the first floor [of a four-story building], a group of students attempted to block this officer from moving down the hallway, creating a melee in which the officer forcefully pushed several students, including one student twice in quick succession" (p. 5). This was the primary example of the use of excessive force documented in the report. (The officers were also accused of using pepper spray, but the report concludes that while one of the officers "brandished

continued

his pepper spray," no one actually used it. Nor was there any evidence of any of the officers punching any of the students, according to the report.)

6. The report also notes that the Department of Public Safety did not adequately prepare the officers for the search. The officers did not clearly and consistently communicate the purpose of their presence. (Many students interviewed by the investigators said they did not know the officers were attempting to investigate a bomb threat, although the officers claimed they signed "bomb threat" at the beginning of their encounter with the students.) They were poor signers, in any event, and no interpreter accompanied the officers in their search.

7. In sum, while finding significant fault with the Department of Public Safety, especially concerning communication problems and the lack of an interpreter, Eric Holder and the other authors of the report (Benjamin J. Razi and Robert A. Zink) clearly did not accept the students' argument that they had a right to occupy the building and consequently were "justified in bumping, pushing, yelling at, and otherwise provoking the officers" (p. 7). In fact, the report states that "we have concluded that the officers, for the most part, performed well under very difficult circumstances" (p. 31). Nor was there evidence that, in a legal sense, the officers used excessive force.

After the Arrests

Throughout October, national leaders of the Deaf community, including leaders of the Gallaudet alumni association and the NAD, pleaded with the Board of Trustees to "do something" to resolve the crisis on campus. Letters from these leaders, as well as their remarks on campus, generally supported the protesters; in fact, many alumni were among those who were arrested.

Many faculty members were also involved in the activities that took place on campus in October. Faculty actions included various informal efforts, both individual and collective, in support of the protest as well as more formal actions taken by the university faculty and by elected faculty leaders. On October 11, for example, "faculty leaders tried to hand-deliver a letter to Fernandes and then e-mailed it to her. 'Gallaudet University is in crisis,' the letter said, and the faculty leaders appealed to her to resign as president designate."[12] In what was reported to be one of the largest turnouts ever for a faculty meeting, on October 16 more than 80 percent of the faculty voted in support of a resolution demanding that Fernandes either resign or be removed. (A similar resolution in May garnered the support of about 68 percent of the faculty.) A week later, the faculty "voted to recommend investigating the presidential search process; ask for an independent mediator; ask for term limits and periodic evaluation of the president; and increase the sign language requirement for tenured faculty."[13] In addition to these activities, a number of faculty members joined about two thousand other people, including many alumni who had come to the campus for homecoming, in a march to Capitol Hill on Saturday, October 21. The night before the march, "a group of faculty members wore academic robes and held a candlelight vigil to underscore last week's vote of no-confidence in the board and Jordan."[14]

While the protesters garnered most of the headlines, a number of faculty and students on campus (some of whom called themselves the Concerned Students of Gallaudet University) attempted to stage a counterrevolution. In one example, a "group of students and faculty and staff members announced yesterday [Thursday, October 19] that it had collected 300 signatures on a petition calling for a return to education at Gallaudet. One student . . . said one of his professors had missed seven consecutive class sessions."[15] Some professors attempted to hold classes at various locations on campus, but, for the most part, these efforts were ineffective, especially because many students were not attending any classes at all, there was no access to the library, computer and science laboratories were closed, and so on.

Many mainstream newspapers and magazines did not support the protest either, unlike the situation in 1988, when a sizeable number of such publications supported the goals of DPN. Several editorials in the *Washington Post*, for example, voiced strong support for Fernandes and encouraged protesters to stop demanding that she step down. On Tuesday, October 10, in an editorial entitled "Standoff at Gallaudet: The Wrong Way to Shape the University's Future," the editorialist wrote: "Ms. [*sic*] Fernandes, well qualified in every way, faces an unenviable job. That she still wants to do it should be one reason to give her a chance."

—*um*—

After several weeks of protest-related activities that essentially shut down the university, coupled with the relentless resolve of many of the protesters that they would not stop until their demands were met, the Board of Trustees gradually began abandoning its heretofore unanimous support for Jane Fernandes. About a week after the arrests took place, the *Washington Post* reported that "Fernandes said some members of the board of trustees have asked her to resign."[16] And, an article in the *Post* the next day reported that "the Board of Trustees has split, with one group backing Fernandes, a slightly larger faction believing she must step down rather than take office in January, and several undecided or whose position is unknown."[17]

Although there may have been some pressure from the board for her to step aside, Jane Fernandes continued to insist that she was the right person for the job and would not back down. In early October, Fernandes was quoted as follows: "Fernandes said she is the only one who can lead the school into the future and make it more inclusive for all types of deaf people. 'I don't think there's anyone on earth who knows the issues better than I do. I've been living in it. . . . I know there's audism here. I know there's racism here. I know it happens, and more importantly, I have a plan to address it.' "[18] Later, she said: "I wish the protesters could give me a chance, because we could do amazing things together. But I have to say this: I *will* be president" (italics in original).[19] Comments like this, while clearly expressing her resolve to stay the course, prompted others to respond with incredulity. For instance, in a October 11 (6:45 p.m.) press release, "a coalition of concerned faculty and students" wrote that the group was "shocked and aghast that Dr. Fernandes still believes that she can lead the university."

Finally, on Sunday, October 29, in an off-campus meeting, the board officially reversed its position and decided to terminate Fernandes's appointment. This decision was widely applauded by many people on campus, especially those who, according to another front-page article in the *Washington Post* the next day,[20] were prepared for more action: "On campus, protest leaders were already promising a new blockade at 6 a.m. today [Monday] if the board did not reject Fernandes."[21] The sentiment of the protesters perhaps was best expressed by the words on a bedsheet displayed on a house across the street from the campus: "First they ignore you, then they ridicule you, then they arrest you, then you win!"

Cultures of Solidarity

One useful way to describe the protest at Gallaudet is to see the protesters and their supporters as exemplifying what sociologist Rick Fantasia calls "cultures of solidarity."[22] Focusing on working-class people, Fantasia examines the ways in which they create various values, norms, and other elements of culture in their search for social justice. In particular, he describes how various aspects of culture and class consciousness (that is, a realistic awareness of their situation vis-à-vis capitalists or employers) emerge during their collective struggles. For working-class people, workplace strikes are the most dramatic example of such struggles, and Fantasia examines how cultures of solidarity are established in these conflicts. He also describes how the cultures of solidarity that develop in earlier struggles (or early phases of one larger-scale effort) can lead to and support future actions. Fantasia argues that "cultures of solidarity are . . . cultural formations that arise in conflict, creating and sustaining solidarity in opposition to the dominant structure" (p. 19).

More generally, cultures of solidarity can develop whenever the usual, taken-for-granted aspects of everyday life are disrupted by those in a position to challenge the status quo. Cultures of solidarity, or cohesiveness, thus exist in opposition to "the way things usually are," and the people involved in such efforts typically seek to promote fundamental social change or social justice.*

Clearly, for many protesters at Gallaudet, their actions were frequently couched in terms of what they saw as an effort to achieve social justice. This was apparent in some of the first letters written to the search committee and the Board of Trustees immediately after the names of the three finalists were made public. It also became apparent when some of the protesters explicitly and implicitly appropriated the spirit of DPN, which achieved its legitimacy when it was perceived as a civil rights struggle, a campaign for social justice.[23]

There were numerous examples of protesters appropriating the spirit of DPN during the 2006 protests. Many of the younger protesters, especially students who had missed out on the events in 1988, felt that it

---

*For Fantasia, the term *culture* is defined broadly and includes characteristics not normally thought of when describing the culture of a group or society. For example, when he describes a strike by the Teamsters Union in Minneapolis in the mid-1930s and the solidarity that emerged during this strike, which helped lead to a victory for the union, he notes the following: "Mass meetings were conducted nightly, and elaborate communication networks were established to keep strikers and supporters aware of developments" (p. 21). If one were to substitute "protesters" for "strikers" in this sentence (and perhaps include cell phones and portable pagers as examples of devices that enable "elaborate communication networks"), one would have an accurate description of some of the organizational activities that took place during the 2006 Gallaudet protest and facilitated its ultimate success.

was now their chance, as well as their responsibility, to "save Gallaudet," as one protesting student (who, like some of his classmates in one of my courses, missed more than a month of classes in fall 2006) said to me. Another example of the spirit of DPN was the phrase "Better President Now," which appeared on campus almost immediately after Fernandes's appointment was announced (and the letters of which— BPN—are written on the stomach of one of the protesters in the photograph on page 187). However, it was not only the spirit of DPN that was appropriated. Some actions, such as Commerson's intervention in the auditorium immediately after the announcement of Fernandes's selection, the use of vehicles to block the entrances to the campus, and the establishment of an ad hoc organizational structure (i.e., FSSA) to coordinate events, also had antecedents in 1988 (when the Deaf President Now Council served a function similar to that of the FSSA). So did one of the demands made by the 2006 protesters: that there be no reprisals against anyone participating in the protest.

Even if one questions whether the protest was fundamentally about social justice, many protesters clearly saw it that way and behaved accordingly (the ubiquitous definition of the situation again). Moreover, when one believes that such a monumental struggle is taking place, perhaps it is a little easier to ignore inconvenient rules and laws in the quest for success. Was this a case of civil disobedience?

Civil Disobedience and Other Aspects of Culture

The issue of civil disobedience came up often during the protest and was used by some of the protesters to explain why they felt it was permissible to ignore the rules and the law in pursuit of a higher goal. This claim eventually led to a brief rebuttal paper, distributed in mid-October on "Inside Gallaudet" by the university administration, about what civil disobedience actually means. This paper was written by Jane Hurst, the chair of Gallaudet's Department of Philosophy and Religion. In this document, entitled "On Nonviolence and Civil Disobedience,"

Hurst observes that historically nonviolence and civil disobedience, as practiced by people such as Mahatma Gandhi and Martin Luther King Jr., go together. She notes that "civil disobedience is a technique of breaking the law and being arrested to achieve a goal." In this scenario, a nonviolent protester who breaks the law, as many people did during the civil rights movement, accepts the consequences of the behavior and willingly pays the penalty. A no-reprisal demand is not the first, or even the second, thing that such protesters insist upon. Moreover, Hurst points out that because many aspects of the Gallaudet protest were not nonviolent, the attempt by some protesters to justify their actions by appealing to the philosophy of civil disobedience lacks a certain logic.*

If one of the aspects of culture that emerged in the protest was civil disobedience, even if it was arguably a rather innovative interpretation, what other cultural characteristics helped build solidarity among the protesters? One important cultural belief that evolved between the start of the protest in May and its climax in October was that the end—getting rid of Jane Fernandes—justified the means. Many people subscribed to this notion in May (and probably before that), and it had become even more important by the fall. If they had to "destroy the village—the university—in order to save it," so be it. (Some protesters used phrases such as this.)

Another aspect of the culture that emerged during the protest was the strong belief expressed by many protesters that Jane Fernandes was not a capable administrator and had not performed effectively as provost.

---

*To be fair, many of those who were arrested on Friday, October 13, were willing participants, especially since they were all released almost immediately after paying a small fine, and many were back on campus the next day. As Susan Kinzie and Mary Otto noted in the *Washington Post* on October 15 ("Gallaudet Reopens with Protesters Still at Front Gates"): "After a night spent on mats at a police training academy, released students wrote their booking numbers on T-shirts, converting them into badges of pride." If these arrests had been followed by a lengthy incarceration, as was the case for many protesters engaged in civil disobedience in the 1950s and 1960s, perhaps fewer people would have been as eager to go through the arrest and booking process in 2006.

Although, of course, some believed this before May, it took on an added dimension during the protest when people were searching for ideological justifications for their actions. Certain aspects of her personality, such as her alleged aloofness and unfriendliness, also took on ideological dimensions as the weeks wore on. In addition, many people believed she was insufficiently immersed in Deaf culture to effectively represent Gallaudet University. In other words, she was not "Deaf enough." Although some of the protest leaders, particularly certain members of the faculty, strongly objected to the characterization of the protest in these terms, the fact remains than many protesters did articulate their concerns by using this rationale. (This was especially evident on some of the blogs—one of the "elaborate communication networks" as it were—that emerged during the protest.) Another belief that emerged to help build cohesion among the protesters was the notion that it was a peaceful protest and that, if there was any violence or if anyone was injured, it was largely the administration's fault.

Another tent city in the atrium of Hall Memorial Building, October, 2006
(Photograph by Barbara White. Used with permission).

In addition to these beliefs, disrupting or not attending classes for weeks on end in the fall, destroying property, occupying buildings, behaving in a way that ignored the legal authority of the Board of Trustees, disrupting campus events, and otherwise disregarding many of the traditional standards of discourse in academia were some of the standards of behavior (norms) that acquired legitimacy during the demonstrations. Whether one sees such actions as a "good thing" or a "bad thing" obviously depends on whether one supported the general goal of the protest. That emerging norms like these led to a number of immediate and negative consequences for the university as a whole, however, is beyond dispute.

One such negative consequence was a decrease in the number of students in the years following the protest. In a presentation to the campus community on September 23, 2008, the president of Gallaudet, Robert Davila, estimated that the university had lost approximately 400 students during the past five or six years. A few days later, in an article in the *Washington Post*, Paul Kelly, the university's vice president for administration and finance, was quoted as saying that during the past five years the university's undergraduate enrollment had "declined from about 1,400 to just under 1,000."[24] Although some of this loss predates the protest, there is little doubt that much of the reduction is a direct or an indirect result of the 2006 protest. In fact, the *Washington Post* reported that the university's undergraduate enrollment was a little more than 1,600 in 1994 and approximately 1,200 in the fall of 2006;[25] thus, in fourteen years, from 1994 to 2008, the undergraduate enrollment decreased by more than 600 students. Another negative consequence of the protest is the fact that the university was placed on probation by the Middle States Commission on Higher Education in June 2007 (a decision that no doubt played an important role in the university's declining enrollment). Following major revisions to the undergraduate general studies curriculum, the development of a new university mission statement, and a renewed commitment to freedom of speech and other forms of well-established academic discourse that were widely ignored during the protest, the university regained full accreditation in June 2008.

What Is There about Gallaudet?

Although a culture of solidarity clearly emerged among the protesters and helped support their objectives, the questions posed at the beginning of this chapter still linger: Why did so many people react as they did to Fernandes's selection? What is there about Gallaudet that seems to encourage an unconventional or confrontational response as the first rather than the last step?

First, it is instructive to compare what happened at Gallaudet with what happened at another university not too far from Washington, D.C., during a controversy related to its president: The College of William and Mary (W&M) in Williamsburg, Virginia. In February 2008, the W&M Board of Visitors fired a popular president who had been in office for about three years. He was apparently too liberal for some alumni and some Virginia politicians. (W&M is a public university.) Among other sins, he moved a cross in the college chapel to a less conspicuous location. According to my son Andy, a W&M graduate, the president probably could have been a better administrator, but many students and faculty liked him and did not want him dismissed. However, after the board's decision, students and faculty did not stage a rebellion, they did not close down the campus, campus buildings were not taken over or damaged, and there were no arrests. They did have a candlelight vigil and put Valentine's Day cards under the ousted president's front door. Life goes on, even if it is not always fair and even if we sometimes don't get what we want.

I suggest that part of the explanation of why an unconventional or confrontational approach seems to be more frequent at Gallaudet than at other institutions is because the university is much more than a school. The ninety-nine-acre, fenced-in Gallaudet University campus is in some ways closer to Vatican City than our counterpart in Northeast

D.C., the Catholic University of America. In many ways, we on the search committee were not so much in the business of selecting a new university president as choosing a new "pope."

The analogy to the selection of a pope is imperfect but useful. For one thing, unlike a university, the Catholic Church does not generally practice shared governance in the selection of its highest officials. Nevertheless, there is a widespread expectation that the leadership roles expected of Gallaudet's president include activities that are not usually associated with university presidents. As one of the most important leaders of the Deaf community, Gallaudet's president serves many cultural, political, and social functions as well and is typically perceived as one of the world's most visible spokespersons for deaf (especially culturally Deaf) and hard of hearing people.

Whatever else Jane Fernandes might be (including, now, the provost and vice chancellor for academic affairs at the University of North Carolina, Asheville), her oral upbringing and tenuous ties to many people in the Deaf community made her insufficiently pious to be a pope. In addition, the fact that many people saw her as cold and aloof made it easier to say that she was not the appropriate person for the job. It is not enough to say that she was rejected; it is more accurate to say she was excommunicated.

―――

Perhaps another explanation for the mass reaction in 2006 is that many Deaf people have become quite concerned about the future of the Deaf community. This concern, which has probably increased since DPN, may help explain why there was perhaps even more anger and emotion in 2006 than in 1988. For example, the number of students in residential schools for deaf students is much less than it was a few decades ago. According to the Gallaudet Research Institute's Annual Survey of Deaf and Hard-of-Hearing Children and Youth, which monitors this on an annual basis, only about 25 percent of deaf and hard of hearing students are now educated in these traditional breeding grounds of Deaf culture (compared to the approximately 55 percent educated in either residential schools or day schools for deaf students in the mid-1970s). Many deaf students today are in some type of mainstreamed educational setting. One consequence of this transformation is that Gallaudet University is now the primary agent of socialization for many people into the Deaf community. In addition, approximately one hundred thousand children around the world (overwhelmingly in wealthy nations) have received cochlear implants. Many people in Deaf communities in the United States and abroad are worried about what will happen as a consequence of this technological development. Many of these children, particularly the increasing number who receive implants at a very young age (including a rapidly increasing number who are receiving bilateral implants), are not likely to be a part of a signing Deaf community in the future.

The most persistent criticism that protesters made during spring and fall 2006 was that the presidential search process was flawed and therefore the result was both unacceptable and illegitimate. Although I have tried to understand their arguments, and agree with a few of their criticisms, I continue to believe that the process was fundamentally fair and certainly much more transparent than some of the critics allege.

As far as the criticisms are concerned, it is unfortunate that the committee got off to a rather slow start in fall 2005. Unfortunately, given the nature of the academic calendar, as well as logistical problems in getting everyone on the search committee to campus (some Board of Trustee and alumni members lived far from Washington), it was difficult to get much done during December 2005 and January 2006. This led to a bit of a rush at the end and may have given the impression that the committee was unable to function effectively. Perhaps we should have continued to work over the summer, but there was a great deal of pressure for the Board of Trustees to announce their decision in May. It is certainly possible that we could have gotten started more quickly if the search committee had been smaller.

The criticism of a "lack of diversity" among the finalists is one that I cannot accept, and I know of no other member of the committee who would accept this criticism either. The fact that the final three candidates were all white does not mean that candidates of color were overlooked. In fact, the exact opposite was the case. I'm sure I speak for others on the search committee when I say that we very much wanted to include a person of color among those we recommended to the Board of Trustees. However, based on all aspects of the screening process, including the candidates' résumés, letters of recommendation, and interviews, the three finalists were the ones that stood out.

I do not violate the integrity of the search process when I say that I personally was not thrilled that the Board of Trustees made the decision to select Jane Fernandes. However, because the process was fair and inclusive, the decision should have been allowed to stand. Obviously, it was not, and I lost respect for many faculty colleagues during the subsequent events: not because they disagreed with the decision, which they had every right to do, but because of some of their actions.

The 2006 protest at Gallaudet, however successful it might have been in terms of achieving the protesters' immediate goal, has not approached the revolutionary impact or near-mythical status accorded DPN, nor is it likely to have an impact beyond Gallaudet. Even that impact is still unresolved. Although university organizational, curricular, and visionary issues have been raised and addressed in the years immediately following the protest (largely in response to the university's probationary accreditation status), lingering resentments remain. A few are worth noting: As mentioned earlier, a significant minority of the faculty as well as a number of students did not support the protest, especially in the early stages. Their voices were drowned out in the effort to convince the Board of Trustees to change its mind. Little has been done subsequent to the protest to deal with the consequences of this "my way or the highway"

approach. Related to this, in spite of assurances that those who broke the law or destroyed university property would be held accountable for their behavior, nothing has been done in this regard; such disruptive behavior was simply ignored in an effort to "put it all behind us."[26] Nor was there any accounting of how much the protest actually cost the university (in terms of dollars, not to mention reputation in the higher education community). The most recent presidential search was concluded in fall 2009, and T. Alan Hurwitz, a former president of the National Technical Institute for the Deaf in Rochester, N.Y., was appointed as Gallaudet's tenth president, effective January 2010. A peaceful transition to the new administration has taken place, and one hopes that the university will not soon be faced with another disruptive and divisive protest.

Some Personal Observations

In the preface, I wrote that in some ways the Gallaudet protest of 2006 represents a continuation of the story of one person's never-ending navigation among several conflicts and challenges: deaf versus hard of hearing versus hearing, American Sign Language (ASL) versus English versus bilingualism, and deaf enough versus not deaf enough. In the first chapter, I mentioned that I grew up as a child with a moderate hearing loss, although I seem to have been a hearing infant and toddler. Later, I developed a more significant hearing loss and, today, without using my cochlear implant, I am a deaf person. I started learning ASL (or at least SimCom, the simultaneous method of communication) when I was thirty, and although I would not claim to have native ASL fluency, I am a reasonably skilled and competent signer. English is my native language, and I strongly endorse the basic premise of bilingualism: fluency in two languages with each language having equal importance and legitimacy. For those who work and study at Gallaudet, this means fluency and competency in both ASL and English.

In recent years, especially since the protest of 2006, the phrases *deaf enough* and *not deaf enough* have been bandied about as shorthand, and not very flattering ways of describing one's level of attachment to the culturally Deaf community. As I mentioned earlier in this chapter, some questioned the appointment of Jane Fernandes as Gallaudet's ninth president on precisely this point, arguing that she should be rejected because she was not deaf enough to lead the university (partly because she did not learn ASL until she was in graduate school). Others, however, insisted that other factors, such as her administrative skills, were more relevant.

In any case, even without the protest of 2006, a heightened emphasis on identity politics, that is, "a wide range of political activity and theorizing founded in the shared experiences of injustice of members of certain social groups,"[27] has become a defining characteristic of many people within the Deaf community. This is true for organizations such as the Deaf Bilingual Coalition and Audism Free America, which were mentioned at the end of the second chapter.

Another recent manifestation of the importance of identity politics in the Deaf community focuses on the concepts of Deafhood and Deaf gain. According to the Innovation Lab at Gallaudet University (gallaudetinnovationlab.org/deafgain.html), the concept of Deaf gain "reframes deafness from the traditional notion of hearing loss to that of deaf gain. From this perspective, deaf people are not defined by what they lack but by their highly visual, spatial, and kinetic ways of knowing and communicating. In this light, Deaf people and their signed languages offer vital contributions to the cognitive, cultural, and creative dimensions of human diversity." Deafhood, too, is a concept that focuses on the positive aspects of being a Deaf person rather than seeing such an individual as a hearing-impaired person or a person with a hearing loss. Although these specific concepts are of relatively recent vintage, they have historical antecedents. During the 1988 DPN protest, for example, there was considerable emphasis on Deaf pride and Deaf power, and a sign was frequently used during that protest to denote the latter: an open-palm hand covering one ear and the other hand raised in a fist. For whatever reason, this sign failed to catch on in the Deaf community, at least at Gallaudet.

There is much that is positive about these developments, including the research that has been done in recent years, especially the VL2 project at Gallaudet and bilingual educational programs established at schools such as the California School for the Deaf in Fremont. One new area of research that has not, as far as I am aware, been extensively explored by researchers who are focusing on learning and language development via visual rather than auditory channels is called *cultural neuroscience*. This emerging field focuses on how cultural factors, including the mores and values of a culture, as well as our experiences have an impact on actually changing or shaping the brain. To the extent that this happens, it would be logical to surmise that a culturally Deaf person might use a different region of the brain to learn language than a hearing person might (or even a deaf person who is not part of the Deaf community). This clearly would have implications for how Deaf children might be taught language and other skills necessary to prosper in a society where a high level of competence in reading and writing English is a basic prerequisite for occupational success.

Although there are many positive developments on the horizon, readers who have made it this far may have noticed that I have repeatedly used phrases such as *a person with a hearing loss* to describe myself (although I don't like and have not used the term *hearing impaired*). Even after teaching at Gallaudet for more than three decades, and even with many Deaf friends, it is a bit difficult for me to get a handle on the notion that this loss is in fact a gain. Moreover, if I saw Deaf gain as something that applied to me personally, why would I get a cochlear implant or even use a hearing aid? More generally, would it be possible for a person with a cochlear implant to identify with the "Deaf gain movement" without experiencing an emotionally unhealthy level of cognitive dissonance?

My personal resolution to the various conundrums that I've experienced or observed over the years can be resolved, at least in my own mind, by looking at the issues on two different levels. On one level, which might be called an intellectual or objective level, I support the effort to develop pride in one's culture and to communicate and learn a language in ways that make full use of a sense (sight) that a person has rather than one (hearing) that a person, to one degree or another, doesn't have. This is especially true for those who do not have a cochlear implant or do not have enough residual hearing, even with a hearing aid, to effectively learn a language by hearing it spoken by others.*

In a paper for the first Deaf Way Conference, held in Washington, D.C., in July 1989, I wrote that it was "simply unconscionable in this day and age" that many deaf children were not being adequately prepared for high-level and high-paying analytical jobs.[28] Although I am hardly the first person to have made this observation, it is a significant issue that is still with us today. Given the unstable economic climate that characterizes the United States at the beginning of the second decade of the new millennium, this may become even more of an issue in the years immediately ahead. As a recent article in the *Atlantic* magazine makes clear, in this new era of relatively high unemployment, for every available job in the United States six people are looking for work.[29] In such a climate, inadequately prepared aspirants will face huge obstacles. Moreover, evidence suggests that "50 percent of 18-year old deaf and hard-of-hearing students read below the fourth-grade level (equivalent to a hearing 9-year-old), compared to about 1 percent of their hearing peers."[30] These results are still unconscionable, and fortunately many researchers are focusing on this problem. Their efforts should be strongly applauded and encouraged.

On a more personal level, I spend most of my time in the hearing world interacting with people who do not sign or are not fluent signers,

---

*Of course, learning the rudiments of a spoken language like English by hearing and overhearing one's parents and others is not the same thing as literacy. Millions of adults in the United States, the vast majority of whom are presumably not deaf or hard of hearing, are functionally illiterate. This is a major social problem that impacts everyone.

so it makes sense for me to try to understand them as well as I can (and, at the same time, do what I can to make the listening environment more positive and productive). In addition, I don't have a particular problem about leaving the question of whether I'm deaf or hard of hearing, or whether I'm part of the Deaf community, or whether I'm deaf enough unresolved. Former New York Yankee catcher and amateur philosopher Yogi Berra has been credited with the following bit of wisdom: "I came to the fork in the road and took it." In my case, I'm deaf and hard of hearing, depending on whether I have my implant on or not. When I'm communicating and associating with my Deaf friends and colleagues, I feel a strong sense of connection with the Deaf community. When I'm with my family and hearing friends, I feel a strong connection with them (especially my family). Like a naïve yet pragmatic patron at a fancy French restaurant, I am not choosy about which forks I use. Maybe this "all of the above" approach is not an optimal way of resolving these conundrums, but it works well for me.

Notes

1. There was some ambiguity in the various announcements distributed on the Web and elsewhere about whether a terminal degree was a requirement for the position. This matter is discussed in more detail in my article, "The 2006 Protest at Gallaudet University: Reflections and Explanations," *Sign Language Studies* 10, no. 1 (2009): 69–89.

2. The letters mentioned in this chapter are included in files related to the 2006 protest maintained by the Gallaudet University Archives.

3. The original wording of this phrase is "if men perceive situations as real, they are real in their consequences." W. I. Thomas and Florian Znanecki, *The Polish Peasant in Europe and America* (New York: Knopf, 1927).

4. Susan Kinzie, "New Gallaudet President Met with Protest," *Washington Post*, May 2, 2006.

5. Susan Kinzie, "Faculty Prepare to Take Sides on New President," *Washington Post*, May 8, 2006.

6. Mary Pat Flaherty and Susan Kinzie, "A Conflict on Integrity Surfaces," *Washington Post*, November 9, 2006.

7. Susan Kinzie, "Protests on Campus Increase," *Washington Post*, October 6, 2006.

8. Susan Kinzie and Michael E. Ruane, "Dozens of Protesters Arrested on Gallaudet's President's Order," *Washington Post*, October 14, 2006.

9. Susan Kinzie and Mary Otto, "Gallaudet Reopens with Protesters Still at Front Gates," *Washington Post*, October 15, 2006.

10. Daniel de Vise, "Deaf Advocate Blasts Arrests," *Washington Post*, October 16, 2006.

11. Burton Bollag, "Protesters Shut Gallaudet Campus," *Chronicle of Higher Education*, October 20, 2006.

12. Susan Kinzie, "Student Rebellion Boils Over at Gallaudet," *Washington Post*, October 12, 2006.

13. Susan Kinzie, "District Briefing," *Washington Post*, October 24, 2006.

14. Petula Dvorak, "From Gallaudet to Capitol: A March in Step with History," *Washington Post*, October 22, 2006.

15. Susan Kinzie, "Fernandes Expresses Resolve to Lead Gallaudet," *Washington Post*, October 20, 2006.

16. Susan Kinzie, "Gallaudet Trustees Split on Fernandes," *Washington Post*, October 19, 2006.

17. Kinzie, "Fernandes Expresses Resolve to Lead Gallaudet."

18. Susan Kinzie and Nelson Hernandez, "Protesters Occupy Gallaudet Classroom Building," *Washington Post*, October 7, 2006.

19. Marc Fisher, "A Lonely Voice for Inclusion in a Redoubt of the Radical Deaf," *Washington Post*, October 19, 2006.

20. Susan Kinzie, Nelson Hernandez, and David A. Fahrenthold, "Gallaudet Board Ousts Fernandes," *Washington Post*, October 30, 2006.

21. Some protest leaders were quoted as saying that "they would make sure the next presidential search is more open and did not rule out further action if they don't approve of Fernandes' replacement." (David A. Fahrenthold and Susan Kinzie, "At Gallaudet, Peace," *Washington Post*, October 31, 2006).

22. Rick Fantasia, *Cultures of Solidarity: Consciousness, Action, and Contemporary American Workers* (Berkeley: University of California Press, 1988).

23. John B. Christiansen and Sharon N. Barnartt, *Deaf President Now! The 1988 Revolution at Gallaudet University* (Washington, D.C.: Gallaudet University Press, 1995).

24. Paul Schwartzman, "Gallaudet's New Aesthetic of Openness," *Washington Post*, October 4, 2008.

25. Flaherty and Kinzie, "A Conflict on Integrity Surfaces."

26. This position represented a distinct change from the board's original stance on this matter. The day after the board decided to terminate Fernandes's appointment, Susan Kinzie, Nelson Hernandez, and David A. Fahrenthold wrote the following in

the *Washington Post*: "Last night, student leaders said they met with some board members who said that protesters arrested during demonstrations will not automatically be expelled but that there will be consequences. The board of trustees issued a statement saying that although they respected the right to free speech, 'individuals who violated the law and Gallaudet University's Code of Conduct will be held accountable'" ("Gallaudet Board Ousts Fernandes").

27. This definition of identity politics is taken from the online *Stanford Encyclopedia of Philosophy*, Stanford University, plato.stanford.edu/entries/identity-politics.

28. John B. Christiansen, "Deaf People and the World of Work," in *The Deaf Way: Perspectives from the International Conference on Deaf Culture*, ed. C. J. Erting, R. C. Johnson, D. L. Smith, and B. D. Snyder (Washington, D.C.: Gallaudet University Press, 1994).

29. Don Peck, "How a New Jobless Era Will Transform America," *Atlantic*, March 2010, 42–56.

30. Marc Marschark, *Raising and Educating a Deaf Child*, 2nd ed. (New York: Oxford University Press, 2007), p. 165. This quotation is based on research reported by Carol Traxler: "Measuring Up to Performance Standards in Reading and Mathematics: Achievement of Selected Deaf and Hard-of-Hearing Students in the National Norming of the 9th Edition Stanford Achievement Test," *Journal of Deaf Studies and Deaf Education* 5, no. 4 (2000): 337–348.

Epilogue

ON TUESDAY AFTERNOON, January 12, 2010, Arlene and I became grandparents for the first time. Our son Erik and his wife Shanna gave birth to a beautiful baby girl in a modern, well-equipped hospital not far from their home in Rhode Island, where they are both college professors. Like many of the thousands of babies who were born in the United States that day, Sabine was given a variety of tests, including a test to determine if she has a hearing loss. Infants are routinely given either an auditory brainstem response (ABR) test or an otoacoustic emissions (OAE) test for this purpose. Both of these tests are painless and passive procedures, and Sabine's results indicated she does not have a hearing loss.

About three weeks after Sabine's birth, Arlene and I flew to Providence to meet her for the first time. Erik and Shanna wanted some time with Sabine before the grandparents, both maternal and paternal, came to visit, and we had to schedule our trip around snowstorms that blanketed the Washington, D.C., area with more than two feet of snow. Fortunately for us, because of the storms we were able to spend a few extra, unscheduled, days in Rhode Island before returning to the nation's capital. Other grandparents will not be surprised to learn that we were delighted to have this extra time with Sabine, as well as with her parents, and that we look forward to the years ahead as she develops her own unique personality, learns a language, gives and receives love, and otherwise grows and matures. Her parents are already teaching her some signs, and I look forward to talking and signing, listening and watching, and doing many other things with her as she becomes a toddler, adolescent, and (we hope) not too rebellious teenager.

Sociologists use the term *life chances* to refer to positive opportunities in life that can be enhanced (or diminished) by particular social arrangements or social conditions. One's chance of doing well in school and eventually attending college, for example, can be improved by social arrangements that reward outstanding teachers and support better—and more equitably funded—public schools, and by programs that, directly or indirectly, support two-parent families. In the United States, there are also many contrasts between the life chances of those who have comprehensive and affordable health insurance and access to good health care and those who do not. As an example, if Sabine were for some reason to become a candidate for a pediatric cochlear implant in the future, the fact that her parents have excellent health insurance makes it more likely that she will have access to this technology than would be the case if her parents were uninsured.

Although the contrast in the various life chances of many different social groups in the United States is noticeable and often disheartening, this contrast pales in significance when compared to the differences between the life chances experienced by those in the wealthy nations of the world and those who live in poor nations such as Haiti or the Philippines. For example, less than an hour after Sabine was born in New England, enormous stress was released on the fault line between the Gonave Microplate and the Caribbean Plate, the two tectonic plates that slowly slide past each other near Port-au-Prince, Haiti, causing a massive earthquake. More than two hundred thousand people died, and countless homes, hospitals, schools, office buildings, and other structures were destroyed in Haiti, the poorest country in the Western Hemisphere. Parents and grandparents everywhere want only the best for their children and grandchildren, but because of conditions and social arrangements over which they may have little or no control, these hopes and dreams are difficult to actualize in many parts of the world. Again using cochlear implants as an example, it is rare for a deaf or severely hard of hearing person living in what is sometimes called the "third world" to have access to this technology.

—*mm*—

In the epilogue to *A Quiet World*, David Myers writes that social and psychological research has repeatedly shown that people with a network of friends and family enjoy greater happiness, live longer, and have better health. Although there are other important factors in this regard (people who exercise a lot generally have better health than those who don't, for example), there is no question that social relationships are vital for an individual's emotional and physical well-being. Forming close social relationships is one of the things that a hearing loss sometimes makes it difficult for a person to do. Difficult, but certainly not impossible. Thousands of deaf and hard of hearing people have close, intimate, and satisfying relationships with others in the Deaf community, and thousands more benefit from hearing aids and cochlear implant technology. Many, like me, are fortunate to have both.

In the final analysis, while I'm sure I will continue to have many communication challenges in the future that resemble those I've experienced in the past, I'm also optimistic that I'm better equipped to deal with them today than I was in the days before I learned how to sign or before I got an implant. In many ways, life is a series of choices, and while I've certainly made my share of bad decisions over the years, on the "big ticket" items related to my hearing loss—particularly signing, teaching at Gallaudet, and getting a cochlear implant—I'm pretty sure I made the right decisions. I've also been blessed with a loving and supportive family that has made my sometimes unpredictable journey through life much more enjoyable and satisfying than it might otherwise have been.

Selected Bibliography

Andrews, Jean F., Irene W. Leigh, and Mary T. Weiner. *Deaf People: Evolving Perspectives from Psychology, Education, and Sociology.* Boston: Pearson Education, 2004.

Biderman, Beverly. *Wired for Sound: A Journey into Hearing.* Toronto: Trifolium Books, 1998.

Chorost, Michael. *Rebuilt: My Journey Back to the Hearing World.* Boston: Houghton Mifflin Mariner, 2006.

Christiansen, John B., and Sharon N. Barnartt. *Deaf President Now! The 1988 Revolution at Gallaudet University.* Washington, DC: Gallaudet University Press, 1995.

Christiansen, John B., and Irene W. Leigh. *Cochlear Implants in Children: Ethics and Choices.* Washington, DC: Gallaudet University Press, 2002/2005.

Chute, Patricia M., and Mary Ellen Nevins. *The Parent's Guide to Cochlear Implants.* Washington, DC: Gallaudet University Press, 2002.

Cohen, Leah Hager. *Train Go Sorry: Inside a Deaf World.* Boston: Houghton Mifflin, 1994.

Davis, Lennard J. *My Sense of Silence: Memoirs of a Childhood with Deafness.* Urbana: University of Illinois Press, 2000.

Gannon, Jack R. *The Week the World Heard Gallaudet.* Washington, DC: Gallaudet University Press, 1989.

Higgins, Paul C. *Outsiders in a Hearing World: A Sociology of Deafness.* Beverly Hills, CA: Sage Publications, 1980.

Higgins, Paul C., and Jeffrey E. Nash. *Understanding Deafness Socially: Contributions in Research and Theory,* 2nd ed. Springfield, IL: Charles Thomas Publisher, 1996.

Jacobs, Paul Gordon. *Neither–Nor: A Young Australian's Experience with Deafness.* Washington, DC: Gallaudet University Press, 2007.

Kisor, Henry. *What's That Pig Outdoors?* New York: Hill and Wang, 1990.

Komesaroff, Linda, ed. *Surgical Consent: Bioethics and Cochlear Implantation*. Washington, DC: Gallaudet University Press, 2007.

Lane, Harlan, Robert Hoffmeister, and Ben Bahan. *A Journey into the Deaf-World*. San Diego: DawnSignPress, 1996.

Leigh, Irene W. *A Lens on Deaf Identities*. New York: Oxford University Press, 2009.

Marschark, Marc. *Raising and Educating a Deaf Child*, 2nd ed. New York: Oxford University Press, 2007.

Marschark, Marc, and Patricia Elizabeth Spencer, eds. *Oxford Handbook of Deaf Studies, Language and Education*, 2nd ed. New York: Oxford University Press, 2010.

Meadow-Orlans, Kathryn P., Donna M. Mertens, and Marilyn A. Sass-Lehrer. *Parents and Their Deaf Children*. Washington, DC: Gallaudet University Press, 2003.

Meadow-Orlans, Kathryn P., Patricia Elizabeth Spencer, and Lynne Sanford Koester. *The World of Deaf Infants: A Longitudinal Study*. New York: Oxford University Press, 2004.

Miller, R. H. *Deaf Hearing Boy: A Memoir*. Washington, DC: Gallaudet University Press, 2004.

Myers, David G. *A Quiet World: Living with Hearing Loss*. New Haven, CT: Yale University Press, 2000.

Oliva, Gina A. *Alone in the Mainstream: A Deaf Woman Remembers Public School*. Washington, DC: Gallaudet University Press, 2004.

Padden, Carol, and Tom Humphries. *Inside Deaf Culture*. Cambridge, MA: Harvard University Press, 2005.

Paludneviciene, Raylene, and Irene W. Leigh, eds. *Cochlear Implants and the Deaf Community*. Washington, DC: Gallaudet University Press, forthcoming.

Preston, Paul Preston. *Mother Father Deaf: Living between Sound and Silence*. Cambridge, MA: Harvard University Press, 1994.

Romoff, Arlene. *Hear Again: Back to Life with a Cochlear Implant*. New York: League for the Hard of Hearing, 1999.

Sacks, Oliver. *Seeing Voices: A Journey Into the World of the Deaf*. Berkeley: University of California Press, 1989.

Schwartz, Sue. *Choices in Deafness: A Parent's Guide to Communication Options*, 2nd ed. Bethesda, MD: Woodbine House, 1996.

Scott, Robert A. *The Making of Blind Men: A Study of Adult Socialization*. New York: Russell Sage Foundation, 1969.

Sidransky, Ruth. *In Silence: Growing Up Hearing in a Deaf World*. New York: Ballantine Books, 1990.

Stenross, Barbara. *Missed Connections: Hard of Hearing in a Hearing World*. Philadelphia: Temple University Press, 1999.

Swiller, Josh. *The Unheard: A Memoir of Deafness and Africa.* New York: Henry Holt, 2007.

Van Cleve, John Vickery, ed. *Genetics, Disability, and Deafness.* Washington, DC: Gallaudet University Press, 2002.

Walker, Lou Ann. *A Loss for Words: The Story of Deafness in a Family.* New York: Harper Perennial, 1987.

Wright, David. *Deafness.* New York: Stein and Day, 1969.

Acknowledgments

I AM INDEBTED to many people who have offered their support, insights, expertise, and constructive criticisms at many stages during the course of this project. First and foremost, my wife Arlene read the entire manuscript, offered countless suggestions and clarifications, and encouraged me to keep writing even when I often wondered if my experiences could possibly be of any interest to anyone outside my immediate family (and, sometimes, even to them). She assured me that other deaf and hard of hearing people, as well as their friends and those in their immediate families, could learn something useful and important from reading about the challenges our family has faced, and how we have dealt with them. I hope she is right. (She usually is, as I've learned over the years.)

My three children, Erik, Anders (Andy), and Amanda, also read the entire manuscript and offered many helpful comments and suggestions. Some of them were a bit painful for me to acknowledge, but, like Arlene, they are no doubt on target in their assessments (most of the time, anyway). I want to particularly thank Erik and Amanda for writing two of the short "sidebars" that are included in the book. Erik also suggested a way to make the chapter on the 2006 at Gallaudet fit more logically into the book's overall theme. Both Erik and his wife, Shanna Pearson-Merkowitz, recently minted PhDs, also made a number of helpful editorial and more substantive suggestions. The support, assistance, and love from all of them are gratefully acknowledged. I'm very fortunate to have such a wonderful family, and whatever merit this book has is due in no small measure to them.

In addition to my family, I have benefited enormously from extremely thoughtful comments from some of my colleagues, most of whom I have known and or worked with for a decade or more. Dr. Morrison (Morri) Wong, professor of sociology at Texas Christian University, and I first met as graduate students at the University of California, Riverside, in fall 1973. Over the past four decades, we have read and commented on each other's work, played many sets of tennis (until I stopped playing and moved on to cycling as my sport of preference—if I've done the math right, at the time I stopped playing tennis we had both won exactly half the sets we played against each other), and have often gotten together at various sociological conferences, typically with Arlene and Morri's wife, Janet. Morri provided a number of insightful comments on the first chapter (the only one I asked him to read).

I have enjoyed a very productive professional relationship with Dr. Irene Leigh, a clinical psychologist at Gallaudet, for more than a decade, as we have written a number of articles and chapters, as well as a book about cochlear implants, together. We have also made many joint presentations. We have often read and commented on each other's papers and books (that we didn't write together), and I have benefited immensely from her wisdom and psychologically oriented insights and observations. Irene read and commented on all three chapters. I should note that Irene has some misgivings about the inclusion of chapter III in this volume, especially since it is quite different from the first two chapters. I hope she agrees that the third chapter, extensively rewritten from the version she reviewed, makes a useful contribution to the book.

Dr. Margaret Weigers Vitullo, who was my colleague in the Sociology Department at Gallaudet for many years, also read the entire manuscript and offered an incredible array of thoughtful and pertinent observations and suggestions. I suspect that the revisions I made after reading and thinking about all of her comments are probably not as extensive as she might have preferred, but this in no way detracts from the scope and thoughtfulness of the comments she wrote on virtually every page of the manuscript. Margaret left Gallaudet University in 2007 and is currently the director of the American Sociological Association's Academic and Professional Affairs Program.

Jennifer Yeagle, my long-time cochlear implant audiologist at the Listening Center at Johns Hopkins University, read and offered many suggestions for the second chapter (the only chapter she read). Since I am not an audiologist, I was particularly dependent on her for making sure that my audiology-related comments in the second chapter were accurate (as well as my description of the different types and degrees of hearing loss in the first chapter). She also refreshed my memory of the sequence of many of the events related to my cochlear implant experience that I describe in the second chapter. In addition to reading and commenting on parts of the manuscript, Jennifer has also worked with me over the years fine-tuning the software in my implant so that I'm able to benefit from the device.

In addition to these reviewers, I also benefitted from very thoughtful and thorough comments made by four reviewers on a version of the third chapter that was published in the journal *Sign Language Studies* in fall 2009. Many of the suggestions they made for the journal article have found their way into the chapter on the 2006 protest that is included in this book. I would particularly like to thank my former colleague at Gallaudet, Dr. John Vickery Van Cleve, and Dr. Brenda Jo Brueggemann of Ohio State University, for their comments on a draft of that article. In addition to their comments, Dr. Sharon Barnartt, my longtime colleague in the Sociology Department at Gallaudet, offered some very helpful suggestions, as did Irene Leigh, who, as noted previously, read the entire book manuscript as well. I have been very fortunate to have received so much constructive and thoughtful feedback from so many colleagues over the years, and, again, whatever merits this book might have are due, in no small measure, to their comments and suggestions.

I have also benefitted enormously from the assistance of Ivey Pittle Wallace, the managing editor of Gallaudet University Press. I have worked with Ivey on several books and other projects over the past twenty years or so and can't imagine a more thoughtful and supportive editor. She has helped me clarify what I'm trying to say, given me reasonable deadlines, and otherwise offered the type of support that good editors provide. It has been a real pleasure to work with her over the years. I am also indebted to Deirdre Mullervy, also of Gallaudet University Press, who made a number of helpful editorial suggestions that I've almost invariably accepted, not only for this book but for several previous publications as well. The assistance of both Ivey and Deirdre is most gratefully acknowledged.

In the final analysis, of course, the responsibility for what appears in this book is mine and mine alone. I have absolutely no doubt that the book is much more interesting, and more clearly written, than it would have been without the insights from my family and colleagues, but while they most certainly contributed to whatever success this book might have, they are not responsible for any of its failings.